THE IMMIGRANT

To Linda Duncan, a wonderful
member of our Akega Team -
From: George Karadin~as
5/9/2013

THE IMMIGRANT

FACING LIFE WITH COURAGE

GEORGE KARAMPAS

iUniverse, Inc.
Bloomington

iUniverse books may be ordered through booksellers or by contacting:

iUniverse
1663 Liberty Drive
Bloomington, IN 47403
www.iuniverse.com
1-800-Authors (1-800-288-4677)

ISBN: 978-1-4620-2287-8 (sc)
ISBN: 978-1-4620-2288-5 (ebk)

Printed in the United States of America

iUniverse rev. date: 08/20/2011

In memory of my parents,
Demetrios and Aspasia Karampas

CONTENTS

PREFACE

I have written *The Immigrant: Facing Life with Courage* to document my life growing up as a young boy in a small village in Greece during World War II, coming to America as a teenager after the war, and living the American dream of countless immigrants.

I have documented events, as I remember them, and the pain endured by the people of my village during the Italian and German occupation during World War II and by the Greek civil war that followed. To save our lives during the civil war, my family escaped to Athens in 1946 where we struggled for many years to survive in postwar poverty. In 1950 recurring problems with osteomyelitis, from which I had suffered for nine years, forced my parents to send me to relatives in America to receive proper treatment. Although we all intended for me to return to Greece after treatment, during the many months of recuperation, I became accustomed to the American way of life and decided to make my home in the United States. Attending an American high school and college and later serving in the United States Army gave me an appreciation for my adopted country and its people.

With this book, I want to present my personal journey as accurately as I can, including my fears, sadness, loneliness and happiness. It is my hope that my story will show that perils always exist in life which we must be determined to overcome.

I dedicate this book to my parents who, under very difficult conditions, instilled in me the right values in life, their love for family and friends, and the importance of facing life with courage.

George Karampas
April 2011

CHILDHOOD IN A SMALL VILLAGE

In the Beginning

My life's journey began on July 14, 1934 in the small, mountain village of Kosma in southern Greece. Although my parents lived in the village of Vrontama about fifteen kilometers south of Kosma, every summer my mother always went to her father's house in Kosma to avoid the intense heat that prevailed in Vrontama during the summer months.

My mother's labor and delivery are legendary in Kosma. I was lying sideways, and three days of labor produced no results. Finally, the traveling doctor came to town. Half a dozen relatives tried to hold my mother down on the kitchen table, but she kept sliding off as the doctor tried to pull me out. Realizing that both my mother and I were going to die, the doctor cut her open. When he saw me, I was covered with lacerations, and one of my ears was hanging by a thread. Thinking that I was dead, he tossed me on a pile of rags in the corner and tried to save my mother. Fortunately, one of the women in the room picked me up and noticed that I was breathing. She wrapped me up, placed the ear next to my head and bandaged it. Miraculously, to the astonishment of the doctor, both my mother and I survived. I still have some scars on my face from that ordeal.

Since Vrontama was the home of the Karampas family, my father transferred my birth records from Kosma to Vrontama. And so my life began in the village of my ancestors.

My father, Demetrios G. Karampas, was born in 1901, one of five children born to George and Panayiota Karampas. My mother, Aspasia (Lambros) Karampas, was born in Kosma in 1912, the youngest of five children born to Elias and Margarita Lambros. My Grandfather Karampas was a farmer and my Grandfather Lambros was a butcher. Both of my grandmothers had died before I was born.

1

My parents and I lived with my Grandfather George in his house which was close to the village square. Like most of the houses in the village, it was made of stone with two rooms downstairs and three rooms upstairs. One of the rooms upstairs had a fireplace where my mother cooked. There was no electricity or running water. We used oil lamps for light and filled a metal barrel with water from a well. In the winter we gathered around the fireplace to keep warm.

My father's brother, Uncle John, lived with us also. My father's two sisters visited frequently and stayed in the house. My Aunt Katerina's husband had left her with two young daughters at a young age and the burden of that family fell on my grandfather, my father, and my Uncle John. It was very difficult for my mother to take care of everyone in the house.

My parents asked my mother's sister, Aunt Marigo, and her husband who lived in America to allow us to stay in a house they owned on the outskirts of the village. We moved into that house and we stayed there until 1939. My sister Potoula was born in 1936, and we lived fairly comfortably because by then my father was the manager of a government supply store. My mother was a kind, hard-working lady, and she took the responsibility upon herself to help with my grandfather's housework and laundry. My grandfather and my Uncle John were always invited to our house for dinner, and we ate together almost every day.

In the winter months, my mother's father, Elias Lambros, would come to Vrontama and stay in a small house he owned. As I mentioned, the village of Kosma was on a mountain where it was very cold in the winter, so most of the residents would come down to stay in Vrontama. Then in the summer, people from Vrontama would go up to Kosma to escape the heat. Grandfather Elias had lived in America where he had learned how to be self-sufficient, and most of the time he would cook his own meals. Grandfather Elias was also looking after his brother-in-law Kotso, who was a little mentally handicapped. The only work that Uncle Kotso, as we affectionately called him, was able to do was to drive a mule or a horse for people who needed that service. He also helped my Grandfather Elias with his farming chores. I still remember Uncle Kotso driving the horses that would carry us from Vrontama to Kosma and back. Unfortunately, he became an invalid before the war and died in my mother's arms in 1939.

In my early childhood, our village did not have a doctor. Anyone who needed medical help had to ride a horse to a larger city to receive any kind of medical attention. Even in the larger cities, the doctors did not have the availability of many medications or equipment to properly diagnose illnesses. I was told that when I was still a baby, Aunt Katerina's daughter, my cousin Georgia, was babysitting me while my mother worked in the fields harvesting the olives. When Georgia tried to lift me from the bed, she accidentally dropped me on the floor. After that fall, I cried continuously for several days and could not sleep. Georgia finally told my parents what had happened, and in desperation they took me to Athens to see a baby specialist. There, I was diagnosed with polio, and my parents were told to take me home because the doctors were not able to help me. After my parents took me home, a village practitioner heard of my problem and came to the house to ask if he could try something that might work. After getting permission from my parents, he pulled my arm really hard, and my arm went back into its socket. My arm was simply dislocated, something that the doctors had not properly diagnosed. My mother told me that I slept for over thirty hours after my shoulder was set.

That fall, however, caused another problem that was not detected until much later in my life. When my shoulder was dislocated, it caused severe nerve damage. The concept of physical therapy was not known at that time, so while I recovered from the pain of the dislocation, the nerve damage went unnoticed. After that fall, any activity that required strength I did with my left arm, and everyone in the family thought that I was just left-handed. However, when I started going to school, I preferred to write with my right hand.

A dentist would come to Vrontama once in a while and stay for a week. He set up his equipment on the second floor of a building on the village square, and people with dental problems would go to see him. Before the war, people would pay him with drachmas, but after the war started, they would barter with him. They would give him a chicken for pulling a tooth, or some olive oil, etc. Just as the war ended in 1945, I came down with a toothache, and my father took me to see the dentist who happened to be in town that week. That was a terrible experience! He sat me down and drilled one of my teeth. Of course, there was no electricity. The drill was connected to a pedal that the dentist pushed with his foot to make it turn and drill my tooth before filling it. I must say that dental hygiene, as we know it today, did not exist. My parents reminded me once in the while to put some water with salt in my mouth and then

3

spit it out again. We did not have a toothbrush or toothpaste until I was twelve years old and we were situated in Athens. Even then, we all shared the same toothbrush.

Our New Home

In 1939, when I was five years old, my mother inherited $1,000 from her uncle who lived in America. That was a lot of money for anyone in the village, and my parents decided to buy their own home. The Lyskas family, who were very good friends of my dad, were moving to Athens for better business opportunities that they had found there. They offered to sell their house to my family at a reasonable price, and we happily lived in it until it became a casualty of war in 1944.

When we first moved into the house, my mom was busy cleaning the inside and setting things up the way she wanted them. She also took up the task of cleaning the area next to the house to make it safe for us to play. In the process of doing that, she discovered that around the stone walls of the area were several snakes of various sizes. That did not bother her at all. On the contrary, she went and chopped most of them up with an ax. The ones that tried to get away and were halfway into the cracks of the wall, she pulled out by their tail. Two of the snakes she was unable to pull out, but with her hands she pulled them so hard that they split in two. My mom was a really strong woman who would do anything to protect us. The neighbors always talked about her toughness in dealing with the snakes.

The house came with about one and a half acres of land where my sister and I used to play and invite other children in the neighborhood to play with us. We did not have any toys, but we always invented games to play without them. I still remember something that resembled a ball that we collectively made so we could throw it to each other. We all decided to make that ball with socks that our families had discarded. All of us brought at least one pair of socks, folded the socks into each other, filled the void with dirt, tied the socks on the top and played with it using it as a ball. As children, we took everything in stride and never complained about things we did not have which perhaps other children in the village had. Running and chasing each other was enough entertainment for us. Many times we managed to get hurt by scraping a knee or by getting hit on the head with the ball we had made, but I cannot remember any of us getting mad at anyone else.

Our new house was in fairly good condition with the exception of the outhouse and the front balcony. Indoor plumbing was non-existent in the village, as in all the villages in the area. Indoor plumbing could only be found in the larger cities such as Sparta, Tripoli or Athens. The outhouse was a small three-sided room with a door on the fourth side. In the middle there was a hole resembling a well about ten to fifteen feet deep with a commode-like fixture on the top of it. My mother would go and clean the commode every so often, but the odor was usually present when you got close. Fortunately, the outhouse was located at a distance from the house, and we never had any problem with odor except when we used it. My dad had wanted to build another, bigger outhouse with a better door closer to the house. That never happened because the war started and he had to abandon his remodeling plans.

My dad had another problem with our new house: the door leading into the ground floor of the house. The original owner was a relatively short man, and when the house was built, he made that door to suit him. The women were by nature shorter than he was. My dad knew that every time he walked through that door, he should lower his head in order to avoid hitting the top of the doorframe. However, most of the time, he would forget to lower his head and would hit it, which was quite painful. Every time my mom saw this happen, much to the dismay of my dad, she would break out in hysterical laughter and would remind him to lower his head next time. My dad was not amused with the after-the-fact advice; he would grumble and go about his business. I must say that although my dad would get angry at times, I never heard him use profanity around us, not even at his most anguished moments.

Now that we were in our own house, my parents told us that Agios Vassilis (Greek Santa Claus) would come to our house on Christmas Eve and bring gifts for me and my sister. We were told that we should hang our stockings in front of the fireplace to receive the gifts that Agios Vassilis would bring for us after we went to sleep. That was the first time that we had heard of something like that. So we hung our socks, and in the morning we found that each of us had an apple and an orange in our socks. We really believed that Agios Vassilis had come while we were asleep and were very thankful for the gifts we had received. That was the first and last time that Agios Vassilis visited us, or if he did visit us again, he did not leave us any gifts. My sister and I kept asking our parents why he stopped visiting us. They told us that the war had scared him away, and it had become dangerous for him to come down the chimneys and deliver his gifts. We never questioned what my parents told us because they had told us that they knew him. We continued to believe in Agios Vassilis and continued to hope that someday he would return with gifts for us.

Mom and Dad made this house into a home for us. This is the home that I remember the most because I always remember it as a joyful place to live with my family, enjoying the love of all the extended family and friends who always visited us.

Being Mischievous

I have been told that as a young child I was quite mischievous and that many times I would provoke my mom into punishing me. Punishment from my mom, although painful, never seemed to hurt too much because I knew that I deserved it. The causes for punishment were many: not doing what she told me to do, arguing with her, complaints from the teacher, bothering my sister Potoula, not listening, etc. The punishment was administered with a stick from the nearest olive tree, a long, thin rolling pin, or by her hands hitting me on the legs.

One day I brought my mom to such an exasperation point that she tied a rope around my waist and hung me in the water well in our yard. The well was very deep; the water was about fifteen feet under the ground. She tied the rope to a nearby tree, covered the well and went inside the house. I was really terrified in the dark with my feet touching the water. I cried and screamed in terror for an hour before Mom came out and asked me if I would ever do again the reason for my punishment. Naturally, I promised I would not. She pulled me back up, and I was so thankful that I fell on the ground thanking my mom for getting me out. Knowing that what I had done was wrong, I also got up and hugged my mom telling her "I love you" with her responding the same way. You would think that I would never forget what I did to make my mom hang me in a well, but I really cannot remember. The well, however, I will never forget.

Right before we moved to our new house and before the war started, knowing that the war would bring shortages of everything that we had to purchase from stores, my dad found somebody who sold him a ten-pound bag of sugar. He sent a message to my mother for me and my sister (I was five years old, my sister, three) to go to the store and carry home a few things for the family. When we got there, he gave me the bag of sugar and a dust pan to carry and gave a straw broom to my sister. We were only a short distance from the house when I decided that in addition to the dustpan and the bag of sugar, I also wanted to carry the broom. Bad mistake!! In the process of getting the broom from my sister, I dropped the bag of sugar on the dirt road which was covered with horse manure and chicken droppings. The bag tore and the sugar was suddenly mixed with the dirt. We tried to save the part of the sugar that was still in the bag, and then I swept the dirty sugar onto the dust pan and mixed it with the clean sugar that we were able to save when the bag fell on the ground. Another big mistake!! When we got home, Mom saw what we had done. It was not difficult to determine the blame for all of this. She was so angry that she took off all my clothes and threw me out into the street. The windows from the neighboring houses opened to see what my mom was yelling about with several women looking at me and laughing. Mom did not let me back in the house until my father came home that evening. In my mind, that was the worst and most embarrassing punishment that I had ever received because it lasted for days when other children in the neighborhood would constantly tease me about it. As it turned out, the sugar that my dad had bought was the last sugar that we were able to get for years.

Mom always explained to me why I was being punished and made me promise that I would never do it again. Although I always promised to stay out of trouble, days later the promise would be broken. I must say, however, that even when my mom was punishing me about something that I did or did not do, I always knew that she truly loved me and was punishing me for my own good in order to help me grow up to be a good and respected person. In retrospect, I believe that she accomplished that goal. My dad would get involved in disciplining me only when my mom was unable to catch me and punish me herself. My dad's punishment was very mild compared to my mom's, but his was the one that hurt me the most. He would hit me on the top of my hand with his own hand. For me, that was the severest punishment, and I always tried to avoid that confrontation as much as I could.

My sister, who was two years younger, was much more obedient than I was. But she also would pick arguments with Mom at the most inopportune times. She wanted Mom to do things for her when Mom was busy doing other things. One day, my mom was busy weaving new blankets on the loom, and my sister came home from playing and told Mom that she was hungry and wanted Mom to get up from her work and cut her a slice of bread. Mom told her repeatedly that she was too busy to cut fresh bread for her and to take a piece of hard bread, dip it in water and eat it with feta cheese that was available next to it. My sister continued to ask Mom to get up from what she was doing and give her the bread that she wanted. She started stamping her feet and demanding that she wanted bread until Mom lost her patience. She angrily got up from the loom, picked up an eight-foot bamboo stick that was close by and threatened Potoula with it. Potoula continued her whining, but knowing that she was about to be punished with the bamboo, she started to run with my mother following her with the bamboo stick in her hands. They both ran, one after the other, right through the village square until they reached the supply store where my dad was working. My dad was somewhat overprotective of my sister, and she knew that he would protect her from her mother's fury. But in this case she guessed wrong. Not only was she punished by Mom, but also by Dad who was furious and embarrassed by the chase in the middle of the square where many men were sitting at the coffee houses and laughing at the whole situation. During her punishment by our parents, I happened to walk by the store where I was called in to observe the proceedings. When I saw Potoula crying, I started to cry myself in sympathy. This was something that both my sister and I would do when one of us was being punished. My dad did not like this at all. He turned and gave me his usual slap on my hands, and then we were both crying justifiably. Potoula was taken home and had to wait for food until supper with everyone else.

On Easter Sunday, all the kids in the neighborhood went out in the street with one hard-boiled, red-colored egg in their hands and challenged each other as to who had the hardest egg. The idea was to crack each other's egg. The boy whose egg was cracked on both ends had to give the cracked egg to the boy who cracked it, and he in turn had to eat the cracked egg. One Easter Sunday, somehow I had an egg that happened to be so strong that I cracked the eggs of ten boys. This meant that I had to eat ten eggs within an hour before I had to go home for our Easter dinner. I was accused by the other boys that my egg was made out of wood and that was the reason that I had cracked so many eggs. To their astonishment, I cracked my egg on the cement to prove to them that it was a real egg. My biggest challenge, however, was waiting for me at home. I had to look for a good excuse to avoid punishment. When I went home, I did not look good, and my mother noticed that I kept going to the outhouse repeatedly to throw up and coming back in the house. I finally told her what happened. Surprisingly she did not punish me because I told her that it was her fault because she had given me a very hard egg. Naturally, I managed to amuse her with that comment. She laughed and told me that I could not have any of the delicious Easter dinner that everyone was having. That did not disappoint me too much because I could not eat anything anyway.

In the fall of 1939, my father decided that I should start going to elementary school as an observer, even though I was not supposed to go to school until the following year. He and my mother thought that if I went to school and listened to the teacher and the older children it would help my behavior. The teacher was my father's cousin, and he talked her into allowing me to sit in her classes and listen. Because all the seats in the class were occupied by the real students, my father gave me a small wooden stool, and I started going to school on a daily basis. I went to that teacher's class until the end of the school year before I entered first grade. The only time I missed class was when I was needed to help harvest the olive trees in November through January.

Although I was mischievous, I was also very sensitive and emotional. I would cry easily at the slightest provocation. My sensitivity earned me the nickname "O Giorgis, O Klapsis (George, the Crier)". It seems strange to me now when I think about it that although I had a reputation for crying easily, I was not really afraid during the war. All those times that we had to run for our lives or watch our homes burn or see people killed I accepted as the way life was.

My life was never a routine, but a series of unexpected events some of which I created myself and others that were beyond my or my family's control. I learned early in my life how to cope and survive no matter what life dished out for me.

The Family

Mom and Dad, in my opinion, enjoyed a good relationship. They did not have an arranged marriage, which was very common in those days, but married for love. By present standards, one could make the case that our home was somewhat autocratic because my dad made the decisions about the issues that confronted the family. My mom waited on him hand and foot. Today we would say he was chauvinistic, but that was the culture of the time.

My mother worked very hard. She cooked on an open fire, washed our clothes in the river, cleaned our house and my grandfather's, helped pick the olives in the fields, sewed our clothes, wove our blankets, took care of two children, her husband, her father, her father-in-law, her brother-in-law, and her uncle. During the war, she also took care of a second cousin, an Italian soldier and a little girl from Athens who lived with us for two years. My mom was a very loving person. I always felt secure in her love my whole life. Even when I was living far away, her constant blessings made me feel safe. She had a wonderful sense of humor and a smile and kind word for everyone. She was also a very strong woman. She did what needed to be done whether it was killing snakes or facing the enemy without flinching. Although she worked very hard, she never complained and was always willing to help others. She was a woman of great faith, and I think that gave her strength to face life courageously. She treated everyone as if they were God in disguise.

My mother was a very devout woman who made me and my sister pray in the morning before going to school and in the evening before going to bed. Sunday was the day of rest in our family and not going to church was not an option. We went to church as a family. The Greek Orthodox Church is the state church in Greece. At that time there were hardly any other denominations in the country and certainly none in the villages. I would go to serve as an altar boy; my father would always sit at a place in church reserved for the elders; my mother and sister would stand on the left side of the church which was reserved for women. When Potoula started school, she stood with the rest of the school girls. There were no pews. Everyone stood except for the elders. The women and girls stood on the left side of the church, and the men and boys stood on the right.

On Good Friday, my mother and several other women would cut all the flowers that had bloomed and would take them to church to decorate for Good Friday services. Every year my mother would embroider a special sheet with religious symbols that would be used for a special service on Good Friday.

My dad was a very intelligent man who loved to read and learn about everything. He barely finished the local elementary school because being the oldest male of his siblings, he had to stop and work in the fields to provide for the family. Even when he was going to school, more often than not, he would be pulled out of class to help the family. But he loved to learn, and he read everything that he could find. His knowledge extended to a wide range of topics such as history, literature, world affairs, etc. He developed his knowledge far beyond the education he received in school.

Under different circumstances, I think my dad would have been a good doctor. We did not have a doctor in Vrontama. A visiting doctor would visit from time to time. Many people came to my father to have their blood pressure taken or to have him give them the shots that a visiting doctor had prescribed for them. This saved them from going to another village to have a doctor give them the shots. My father had become quite proficient in doing all this. He had brought the blood pressure equipment from Sparta and would always dismantle the only syringe that he had, drop it in a metal dish, pour some homemade alcohol on it and disinfect it. He never accepted or asked anyone for anything as payment for what he did.

Before the war, there was a youth movement throughout Greece that was sponsored by the Metaxas government to instill patriotism in the youth between the ages of twelve to nineteen. My father was appointed as the leader of the youth in our village. Under his leadership, the youth were given blue and white uniforms which they proudly wore for special celebrations such as Greek Independence Day, Easter, etc. Those youth were basically performing duties that the present-day Boy Scouts would have. They were very patriotic and on holidays they attended church services as a group wearing their uniforms and marching in formation into a special section of the church.

My dad was responsible for running the government store in our area. People would come from surrounding villages to shop there. My dad was well-respected and people came to see him about a variety of things. He would give advice on legal matters and be the go-between in resolving disputes between villagers. My father was recognized by his peers as one of the pillars of our village. He was a very honorable, patriotic man who loved his village very much.

Before he fell and broke his hip, my Grandfather George always rode the best horse that the family had when he wanted to go anywhere. When the family went to attend different festivals, such as St. George's Feast

Day, my grandfather would take me to ride on his horse with him. I was the only Karampas grandson he had, and I think that he wanted to show me off to his friends. The St. George Church was across the Evrotas River, a few kilometers outside of the village. It was small and could only accommodate about thirty people inside. Most of the people who attended the services during the Feast of St. George had to stand outside of the church. My grandfather, being on the church council, always found a way to be inside the church, and he took me inside with him. He took his position on the church council very seriously. He would not allow anyone in the congregation to talk during the Liturgy. He considered it disrespectful and would not hesitate to ask people to leave the sanctuary if they continued to speak.

Before the war, the Feast Day services at St. George Church were always followed by what we called a "glendi," which means a festival of eating good food, dancing, socializing and, for the adults, drinking wine. The area around the St. George Church was flat and was only disrupted by a small stream of water running through it. It was during the glendi of 1940 right before the war that I saw my father having too much wine to drink for the first and last time in my life. He was leading a dancing line with his friends and decided to cross one of the small streams in the area when he was pulled back by the rest of the men in line and fell into the stream. He then pulled everyone else forward and soon everyone was in the water. They all got out of the water totally wet and continued their dancing as if nothing had happened while the rest of the people laughed and made fun of them. This "glendi" was the last such event that was celebrated by the entire village in a very cohesive way where everyone considered everybody else a friend, a neighbor or a relative. Unfortunately, the war and the civil war that followed changed everything into jealousy and hatred.

My Grandfather Elias, when in Vrontama, would never miss any Sunday or holy day church service. I was very happy to be with my grandfathers. I was always conscious of their love for me and always responded well to any of their requests. Unfortunately, Grandfather Elias was diagnosed with throat cancer in 1942, and it became very hard for him to take care of himself as he had been able to do until then. Mom and Dad decided that he should come and live with us so that my mom could take care of him. He was a wonderful man, full of energy and kindness, and I will never forget any of the times that I spent with him.

My Uncle John was the chanter of our church. He had learned Byzantine music from my dad and was thought to be the best chanter in the village.

As for me, I was an altar boy from a young boy. As I got a little older, I learned my duties as an altar boy so well that I became the priest's right hand. As long as we lived in the village, I was with the priest at all the services he performed: weddings, baptisms, funerals and blessing of the homes. I would be in church with Fr. Vassilis from the beginning of the services and would go around to the houses in the neighborhood and ask for coals needed for the censor during the Liturgy.

In the spring of 1946, when I was almost twelve years old, I decided that I was too old to be an altar boy. I had only short pants to wear. I started to have hair growing on my legs, and the robe that I had as an altar boy was getting very short for me. Therefore, I made a unilateral decision, without saying anything to Fr. Vassilis or even my parents, that I would not go into the "hiero" on the following Sunday. (In the Greek Orthodox Church the sanctuary is separated from the altar by an icon screen which has three doors. The area behind the icon screen is called the hiero.) Instead I went and stood with my classmates next to the chanter's stand. When Fr. Vassilis saw me, he came to one of the side altar doors and motioned to me that he wanted me to go and see him there. Reluctantly I went to meet him just inside the hiero. He closed the door, got hold of my ear and pulled me to the area where the altar boys usually stood during the Liturgy. I protested that I was too old to be an altar boy, but he had nothing to do with anything that I had to say. Instead he told me that he would tell me when I was too old and that he wanted me to be an altar boy until he made that decision. If I disagreed with that, he was going to tell my mother. I already knew what my mother would say, so I accepted Fr. Vassilis' decision. I continued to serve as an altar boy just as I had done for years until we left Vrontama.

Many times on Sundays when the men went to the coffee houses in the square after church services, my dad would run into a friend visiting from another village and would invite him to have dinner with us. We children always played in the square after church. My dad would call me over and tell me to go home to tell Mom that we would be having a guest for dinner. My mom had to make due with what she had to accommodate the unexpected guest. She always welcomed visitors in our house. My sister and I were not too keen on having a guest because the dinner table could only be set for the grown-ups. This meant that we would have to sit on the floor and eat. Mom would put down a blanket next to the table and we would sit on it to eat. We did not complain, but we were not very happy about the situation.

My sister and I were very close as children. We were always together. I always thought that I needed to protect her, and when we walked together, I wanted to hold her hand, much to her objection. I also liked to tease her like all brothers do. My favorite trick was to pinch her feet with my toes under the dinner table. She would complain that I was pinching her, and I would innocently deny the accusation because my hands were visible on the table.

My two grandfathers and Uncle John were our permanent guests for dinner. During dinner, my place was between my two grandfathers, who always gave me about an inch of our homemade wine to have with my meal. They, in turn, would jiggle their glasses and toast each other and me several times during dinner. My dad was not much of a drinker, but he and Mom would always have a glass of wine. Potoula was not allowed to have any wine until she was older. Those were the wonderful times that I will always cherish. The house was full of love and laughter. Those were some of the best times of my life.

Laundry Days

Laundry day was a long, full day of work. Mom did the laundry not only for our immediate family, but also for my Uncle John and for both of my grandfathers. I must mention that my mother made all the soap that we needed for our personal use and for the laundry. It took two or three days to make soap from the time the process started to the time the soap would surface on top of the boiling water, harden and then be cut into pieces for use. The soap-making process needed a lot of attention, which meant that some of the daily routines of the maker were neglected. My mother, like most other women, usually asked another woman relative to help when making soap. Aunt Katerina, or Thea Katie as we affectionately called her, was my mother's helper on most of the soap-making days.

Since we did not have running water in the village, Mom would take the laundry to where water was available. We had two horses in the family, and both of them were used to carry the laundry and a big round tub to where the water for the laundry was located. Most of the time Mom would go to a property owned by our family called the "aloni" where there was a well. Other times when the laundry was more than usual, she would go to the Evrotas River which was further from the village. The Evrotas River flows through Sparta, north of Vrontama, and history tells us it was the place where the ancient Spartan warriors would bathe before going into battle with the enemy.

In our pre-school days she would take me and my sister with her for the all-day affair. Mom would bring dried bread, cheese and olives to feed us when we were hungry. My first responsibility for the day was to go around and collect whatever wood I could find to start the fire and keep it burning for the whole day. My mom would take stones and place them around the fire and then place the round tub on top of the stones to heat the water. I would help her fill the tub with water from either the river or the well in the aloni while my mother would separate the clothes, add the soap, and put them into the boiling water in the tub. The rinsing was done with water from the river or from the well, after which the clothes were placed on nearby shrubs to dry. At the end of the day, everything was loaded onto the horses and carried home where the ironing process started the following day. Laundry day was a very exhausting day for my mother. During that day, I helped my mother as much as I could by doing little things for her such as providing wood for the fire, feeding my sister, spreading the clean clothes on shrubs and collecting them at the end of the day so we could take them home. Not only did my mother do laundry for the whole day while looking after me and my sister, but when she came home she was also faced with the task of cooking dinner for everyone.

Now, this did not mean that everyone else was sitting around all day and not doing anything. Everyone had his own responsibilities and daily chores. My father had the work of the government store. Many times when he found somebody to tend the business of the store for a few hours, he would come to where we were and help my mother with the heavy work. My Uncle John was constantly working in the fields, planting wheat seed, pruning the olive trees, clearing brush from our fields, etc. My grandfathers went to the fields and did whatever light work needed to be done.

By present standards, that was a very hard life, but it did not seem to bother us because that was what we knew. We were happy. We accepted our life as it was, and on Sundays we would go to church and thank God for the blessings that were given to us, the love of family, food to eat, and good friends.

My Chores and Daily Life

The aloni is a property of about four acres in the southwest part of Vrontama, about one kilometer from our home. It is located on the top of a hill, but it is fairly level on the top. From there, one has a perfect view of our village, the Parnonas Mountain to the north and the Taiyetos Mountain to the south. Because of its good location, my Grandfather George constructed two circles with cement, each with a diameter of about fifty feet. Those two circles were used during the wheat harvest season. In the center of each circle there was a pole with a ring on top. We would tie a horse to the pole with a rope long enough to allow the horse to walk around on top of the cement circle. We would spread the harvested wheat on the top of the cement and have the horses stomp around the circles until the grain was separated from the straw. After the horses were done, the straw and the grain would be swept to one side of each circle, and with pitchforks the owners of the harvest would pitch the straw into the air separating the straw from the wheat. This process had to take place at about 4:00 P.M. because that was the time that the wind would start blowing to make this possible. Most of the villagers would bring their harvest to the aloni and stack the bundles of their harvest there until it was their turn to thresh it. As compensation for use of the field, the cement circles, and the well that provided them with water, my grandfather would get a very small portion of the harvest. The aloni was also my favorite place to play with my friends. On several occasions such as the first day of Lent, Easter, etc., groups of people from Vrontama would go to the aloni to celebrate by eating and dancing there. Everyone in the village had some kind of memorable occasion that was celebrated at the "Karampas Aloni."

Our family also used the aloni for grazing by our animals. We always had a goat that provided the milk for our breakfast. When I got to be about six years old, I voluntarily accepted to do some of the chores that the adults did not have time to do. My job was to take the goat to the aloni in the morning for grazing and bring it back home before dark at night.

There was always enough vegetation and leftover straw from the threshing of the wheat for the goat to graze. I would tie the goat with a long rope so she would have enough to eat and water to drink during the entire day. A couple of times, when the goat was pregnant, I would go to the aloni to bring her home in the evening and would find that she was in the process of giving birth or that the birth had already happened during the day. I was always fascinated and happy to see this new life. Most of the time, there would be more than one baby. The goat had her own way of giving immediate care to her kids, and within a very short time she had them clean and walking on their own. If any of the newborns were not able to walk home, I would carry them in my arms.

As I mentioned before, we did not have running water in the village, and there was not always enough in our water well at home for watering our horses after a long day's work in the fields. I would ride the horses to the community wells that always had plenty of water. I carried a bucket with me, tied it to a rope that I lowered into the well, filled it with water, pulled it up, and had the horses drink from there. I was always happy to water the horses, not only because I thought of the horses as my friends, but also because I had the privilege of riding to the wells and back home and sometimes racing with other kids who were watering their horses at the same place.

As I got a little older, in addition to watering the horses, I would also be sent by my mother to bring water from the community wells if more water was needed at home over and above what we had available. An adult would mount one water tank on each side of the horse, and I would ride the horse to the wells, water it, and with the help of the same bucket, I would fill both water tanks, seal them on top, and take the horse back home. The tanks were quite large and held about ten to fifteen gallons of water each. When I got home the adults would take over to unload the horse and store the tanks of water for later use.

Late November, December and the first part of January were dedicated to the harvest of olives from the olive trees. Everyone in the family helped in this activity. On non-school days, Mom and Dad would take us with them to the fields to help with the olive harvest. The adults would climb a ladder with a hamper strapped around their waist and strip the olives from the olive branches. My job and that of my sister when she was older was to stay on the ground and by hand collect all the olives that had fallen from the wind, rain and hail. In some cases, because of adverse weather conditions, most of the olives would have fallen on the ground and everyone helped to pick them up. Because the harvesting was done during the rainy season, many times we would be caught in the rain, and we would head for any kind of shelter that we could find to keep from getting too wet. When the rain stopped, one of the adults would light a fire to warm us, and then we would go back to our work. The olives were dumped into large bags which were loaded on the horses and taken home. When it was our family's turn, the olives were taken by a horse-drawn cart to a plant where they were converted into olive oil. Olive oil was a staple in our diet.

After the olives were harvested, it was time for the land to be plowed and seeded with wheat. My father would invite friends to help our family with the plowing and seeding of the fields. We used that wheat to make bread for the whole year.

Sometimes, I had to get up early in the morning in order to walk to the fields with the adults and then ride one of the horses back to be used by the family for other chores. The early mornings in February and March were very cold, and coming home, the ride seemed like an eternity to me. I was freezing riding the horse, and I would try to get warm by leaning forward and hugging the horse's neck. The cold did not seem to bother the horse at all. When I arrived home, my mother would put my hands and my feet in warm water until I felt better. Then she would give me warm milk and an egg and send me to school.

The only type of heat that we had in our house was a wood-burning potbelly stove for the first floor and a fireplace on the second floor. The fireplace was also used by my mother for cooking our meals. My job was to go out in the yard, bring some wood into the house from the stockpile kept there, and start the fire in the fireplace. In addition to cooking, the fireplace was also used as a gathering place after the meal and kept us warm in the winter months. All of us would sit in front of the fireplace keeping ourselves warm, with the adults discussing their own issues while my sister and I would listen. That was also the time that my dad would ask us to tell what we had learned in school that day and if we had answered all of our teacher's questions. If the teacher had problems, mostly with me, I knew that my dad would have already been informed of that by the teacher. It was a small town, and the teachers knew everybody in the village. It was, therefore, in my best interest to be honest and not try to hide anything.

What I enjoyed the most after dinner were the stories that both of my grandfathers would tell us. They talked mostly about their youth, telling stories about working in the fields while being attacked by wild dogs, swimming in the Evrotas River and almost drowning, being mischievous when they were young, etc. That was my favorite part of the day.

My father and mother would tell me and my sister when it was time to go to bed. Actually our bed was the floor with some homemade blankets underneath us and on top of us. Before we went to sleep, we would go around the room and kiss everyone's hand as a sign of respect and love and say good night individually. We had to do this for anyone who happened to be in the house, relative or not. Before sleep we had to say our prayers which our parents taught us and kneel down to thank God for all the good things that we had.

Every year my mom would buy a very young pig from people who came to town selling them. The family had designated her as the person to always buy the pig because she always had the good luck of buying a healthy pig. When we still lived in the old house, the pig was let loose around the yard, and it soon started to dig into the ground messing up my parents' garden. This was unacceptable to my dad. He wanted the pig to stop doing what was natural for pigs to do. So, he enlisted the help of my grandfather and Uncle John to hold down the pig while Dad tried to pierce its nose and insert a ring into the nose. Bad idea! In the struggle the pig opened its mouth and bit Dad almost taking his thumb off and leaving it gushing blood. They let the pig go, and it ran away. We did not see it for days until my mom went looking for it.

Every year before the Great Lent, we had the ritual of slaughtering the pig. The slaughter would always take place in the backyard of my grandfather's home. Here again, the three men would hold the pig down while my Grandfather Elias who was an experienced butcher slaughtered the pig. My job was to pull the pig's tail and keep it straight while saying the Lord's Prayer until the pig was slaughtered. There was not any particular significance to this, other than the adults wanting to get me involved in the process and having a laugh at my expense. When I got a little older, I caught on to their joke and refused to do it any longer.

My parents and grandfathers taught me a lot about life, work, friendships, respect for elders, and love of family. I learned that everyone in the family had a part to play and their own responsibilities that went with it.

Vacations

When I was five years old, my parents decided to take us to a large city for shopping and to give me and my sister the opportunity to see what a big city was like. They engaged the services of one of my dad's friends who owned a taxi to take us to Sparta and the even larger city of Tripoli. In Sparta we visited with my parents' friends. Holding our hands, my dad took us for walks along the main streets of Sparta where I saw paved streets, palm trees, night street lights, and for the first time many cars moving on the road. I was totally fascinated with the entire experience. I saw people well-dressed in the middle of the day, and I asked my dad to tell me why they wore their good clothes to go to work. In the evening, I was taken to an outdoor cinema. We walked into an open place where we could hardly see the chairs where we were supposed to be seated and a large screen showing pictures of people, cars, etc. The pictures were moving and the objects on the screen were changing size: at times they were big and then they would become small. I was fascinated with the whole thing and was asking all kinds of questions until my dad asked me to be quiet because people were turning around to tell us that we were disturbing them. That was the first time that I went to a cinema, and it would be seven years before I went to another.

From Sparta we went to Tripoli which is about thirty-nine kilometers north of Sparta. We visited my Uncle Nick who was a school teacher in Tripoli and married to Aunt Evgenia, my mother's older sister. They were living in a large home owned by Uncle Nick's sister and brother-in-law. That is where we stayed during our visit. The house was located on a busy street not far from the center of the city. I could never get enough of looking at everything that was taking place outside. I stood on the balcony overlooking the street and watched the maids from across the street placing the blankets and rugs on the railing and beating them to get rid of the dust. I was able to look at the circle in the center of the city and see a huge statue of a hero from the Greek War of Independence, Theodoros Kolokotronis. We children had been told about him; everyone always talked about him with respect and admiration.

My mother and Aunt Evgenia took my sister to a department store for some shopping. When Potoula saw a counter displaying earrings, she convinced Mom to buy her a pair. Someone from the store began piercing her ears. She started crying, but when they offered to stop she told them,

"Let me cry, put those earrings in." Later, while walking around the store, Potoula got separated from my mother and got lost. She started to cry and people from the store came to her rescue asking her about her parents, etc. Not knowing where she was or where she was staying, she kept saying that she had a brother named George and she came from Vrontama. The police were called and walked her around the store until she spotted Mom and Aunt Evgenia.

The next day we got a taxi and went through Sparta to the village of Zoupaina which today is known as Agioi Anargyri. This is a smaller village on the way to Vrontama. One of my father's sisters and her family lived there, and we wanted to stop and see them. It was a moonless night, and without any other light, we proceeded to walk up the hill to the house. I fell and hit the middle of my forehead on a sharp stone. Blood started to run down my face, and my father wrapped my head with whatever he could find to stop the bleeding. When we got to Vrontama, Dad had plenty of bandages that he used after he cleaned my forehead. I still have a big scar on my forehead to remind me why I never really liked the village Zoupaina.

That was the only family vacation that we ever had. However, at the end of every school year, our parents would send us to Kosma to live with our Grandfather Elias and my mom's sister Evgenia and her husband for the summer. My father stayed in Vrontama and would come to visit us two or three times during the summer. He was not able to leave because of the government store. Mom also stayed in Vrontama with my Dad but would visit us often. Every week she would send us fruit and fresh vegetables with other people coming to Kosma from Vrontama.

The family was very busy the day before going to Kosma. Mom would prepare the clothes we needed for the summer while my sister and I would go see all our friends in the village and say our goodbyes. In preparation for our trip to Kosma, my parents would send us to bed early while they packed our belongings and got them ready to load on the horses. In order to avoid the heat, we were awakened at 3:00 A.M. When Uncle Kotso was alive, he was the designated horse driver. After he passed away, Dad found others to take us up the mountain. Each horse was loaded on each side with our supplies and with blankets spread over the middle for us to sit. Although the distance was only fifteen kilometers, the terrain between the villages was mountainous with very narrow paths for the horses to walk, especially on the side of the cliffs. I always wondered how the horses were able to find just the right place on these paths to place their feet and avoid tumbling down the mountain with us on them. It was always very peaceful during the trip. The only sounds I was able to hear were the bells strapped around the horses' necks, the driver's voice guiding the horses, and the faraway barking of dogs. When we arrived in Kosma, the sun would be making its appearance on the horizon. After the horses were unloaded, I would take them to the village watering holes. After we let them rest, they were fed plenty of straw and in the evening the driver would take the horses back to Vrontama.

During our summers in Kosma, I made friends with children of my own age who always expected me every year. Besides the kids who lived in Kosma, there were other children who were there just for the summer. There were plenty of activities for kids to do. There is a church in the village square that has three marble lions' heads on one side. Water flows underground and pours out of their mouths. We loved to chase each other through the square and splash in that water. We also loved to explore the mountainsides, finding small caves in which to hide and picking blackberries for eating contests. Sometimes I would not come home when I was told, and my grandfather would go out looking for me. Grandfather Elias was a very mild-mannered man and he never raised his voice to anyone. The only harsh language he would use was, Where in the devil's behind have you been? He spent most of the morning in the coffee house in the square. When my sister and I would see him coming around the bend of the road on his way home for lunch, we would run to him and put our hands in his coat pocket where he always carried two pieces of hard candy for us. We thought that was the best gift each day. When September came around, we headed back to Vrontama for the winter, ready to start a new year of school and resume our childhood activities where we had left off.

Childhood and Family Friends

Almost all of the children in our village were friends. We used to stop by each other's house and make ourselves comfortable playing there or taking off and playing somewhere else with more kids. We knew where everybody's house was and the parents in most cases knew each other. Our security was never an issue with any of the parents, unless we somehow hurt ourselves playing. If we did something wrong, all the parents knew it, and the children had to face the consequences when they got home.

One of my friends who lived in another neighborhood and used to come to ours to play with us was a boy named George. George and I were the same age and in the same class in school. Because we looked somewhat alike, at times people in the village would confuse me for him and vice versa. One time my mother was looking for me for a long time and could not find me. By chance the other George was walking down our street and my mom saw him and ran after him. When she caught him, she grabbed him by the ear and started scolding him. George turned around and told my mother that he was not her George. She felt bad about pulling his ear. Later she told his mother about the incident and they both had a good laugh.

Each neighborhood also had its own little group of friends that played mostly together. In my case, there were many children in the neighborhood and most of the time we played close to home. My father's first cousin lived next to my grandfather's house and had a boy and a girl who were the same age as me and my sister. We were the best of friends and companions. My father's sister Katerina had two daughters, Popi and Georgia. Georgia was the one who dropped me on my shoulder when I was a baby. Georgia and I were birds of a feather.

Although Georgia was older, together we had become pranksters. Most of the time, we played our jokes on Aunt Katerina, perhaps because she was always good-natured towards everyone. She used to sprinkle figs with oregano, spread them out in the sun to dry, and then store them for use as snacks during the winter. The sweetness and aroma from those dried figs did not escape Georgia and me. Her mom would hide those figs and serve them as a sweet only to the guests who came to her house for a visit. She stored them in a little dry well on the ground floor of her house. She kept this hiding place from us because if we knew where the figs were, they would be disappearing faster than she could make them. Georgia and I soon found the hiding place, took some of the figs, ate them and waited for Aunt Katerina to go into the well with a small ladder to get figs to serve her visitors. She saw that most of the figs were gone, and knowing who took them, she started yelling at us. Georgia and I found the cover and covered the well with my aunt in it. Then we placed a bag of flour on the top so that she could not lift the cover and get out. We both left the house. A little later we returned and helped her get out. Naturally, we were both punished when my dad found out what we had done. There were other pranks that we pulled on Aunt Katerina and others in the family, but that was the worst.

Behind my grandfather's house was a beautiful house that belonged to the Katsicopoulos family. Mr. and Mrs. Katsicopoulos and their two children George and Mary came from America in the early 1930s and built the best house in our village. While they were in Greece, they had another girl whom they named Joy. Our families became good, close friends. Their son, George, was very gentle and kind to me, and as I grew a little older, I thought of him as an older brother. I remember that he found some old wheels from a baby stroller on the ground floor of his house. Those wheels aroused my curiosity, and I would use the bamboo bundles in my grandfather's backyard to climb the back wall of his house and ask George a million questions about those wheels. George was trying to make some kind of cart for me. I don't believe that he ever finished it. But he always talked to me and invited me to their home to spend time with him. As I have mentioned, I was mischievous at times, and it was not unusual for me to have to stay after school as punishment. Many times George's sister Mary would bring me something to eat and pass it through the window when the teacher wasn't looking. George was my role model, and our families enjoyed many good times together.

Before the war, my dad and Mr. Katsicopoulos went on a vacation together to the hot baths called Methana. A few times during their absence, George's mom and my mom decided to take all of us children to the aloni to sleep out under the stars. We got so tired that we slept until the sun came up the next day. Knowing that the winds of war were getting stronger and that it was inevitable that war would come to us, George's father decided to return to America and then bring his family after he was settled in Dayton, Ohio. Unfortunately the war started before he could send for them, and George, his mom and his sisters had to stay in Vrontama until the end of the war.

The Katsicopoulos family also used to go to Kosma for most of the summer, and, you guessed it, the house they rented was next to my grandfather's house. We never dreamed during those childhood years that our paths would meet again in America. My life's journey brought me halfway around the world, and surprisingly my oldest and dearest friends came to almost the same place. We still see each other often, living only about sixty-five miles away from each other, and we still consider each other best friends. A few years ago, I attended George's 80th Birthday Party, and I realized that next to his sisters, I had known him longer than anyone in the room. We have come a long way from Vrontama, but I still think of him as an older brother and cherish his and his sisters' friendship. A true, sincere friend is precious, and I have been blessed to have such lifelong friends.

SURVIVING THE WAR

The Start of the War

I was barely six years old on October 28, 1940 when the drums of war became louder and Italy declared war on Greece. My father was thirty-nine years old and my Uncle John, thirty-two when they both answered the call to defend the homeland. Within two days we saw trucks coming to town empty and leaving full of men going to war. I remember the people of my village gathering in the square and singing the National Anthem of Greece with such courage and enthusiasm that one would have thought that they were heading to a big celebration. The activity in the village was unbelievable. People were walking the streets in a hurry, visiting each other's homes trying to collect warm clothes, socks and scarves to give to the men headed for the freezing weather of northern Greece along the border with Albania, Italy's ally at that time.

My father and Uncle John left with everyone else on the trucks, and my mother was left to take care of all of us. My sister and I cried a little seeing my father and Uncle John leaving, but my mother consoled us telling us that they would be coming back soon victorious. Later we learned that my father was stationed in Nafplion which was an army base dealing with logistics and war supplies. We knew then that he was out of danger. Uncle John was assigned to an infantry unit on the Albanian border serving in communications. Later we received a picture of him in a fox hole, covered with ice and trying to operate a wireless radio.

My father's departure left a void in the operation of the government store. My grandfather tried to operate it as best he could. It soon became obvious that he was not able to do it, and my father asked the oldest son of one of his friends to take over. This did help, but soon the supplies were totally dried out. The government was preoccupied with the war, and the transportation of the supplies became non-existent. Later, when Germany entered the war with Greece, the supplies for the government store were taken over by them for their own use.

And so our village and other nearby villages were left without petroleum, salt, fertilizer and even matches. The hard times had come. Greek money was worthless. I remember people going to a store with a suitcase of money to buy a small amount of food for their families. After a while, no amount of money was accepted by anyone.

The Greek army fought the Italians in northern Greece, and their heroism was legendary in the entire free world at that time. Mussolini's forces were pushed back to Albania and then to the Ionian Sea. They were humiliated in the eyes of the world and a disappointment to Hitler who expected the Italians to take Greece quickly on their own so his forces could be utilized on other fronts. Hitler had to intervene with his own forces. The German army, supported by its air force and armored divisions, invaded my country and supported the Italians in their goal of occupying Greece. The Greek army, although greatly outnumbered, fought the Italians for more than seven months.

The German army came to Italy's assistance, and the Greek army fought them for over two months with such bravery that it attracted the attention of the leaders of the free world and even Hitler himself. The enemy conquered Greece but not the Greek spirit. The Greek soldiers did not surrender but returned home with their heads up and proud of what they had done. My father and Uncle John returned from the war and were ready to fight another one for our liberation. At the beginning, the Italians were the primary occupying force in our village and other villages in the southern part of the Peloponnese. The Italians were the primary target of the Resistance in our area.

The Italian Occupation

The Italian army moved into our village at the beginning of 1941 and set up their headquarters in one of the buildings on the village square. Those soldiers stayed in our village until the end of 1942 when Italy quit the war. The people of the village continued to go out to their fields and work the land, harvest the olive groves, seed the fields with wheat and in the spring plant their vegetables down at the river banks. This only lasted for a short time because the Italians started to take most of what was produced for their own use and sent the rest to their headquarters in Sparta to support their army there. They methodically started taking a little, and as time progressed, they took more and more. This resulted with the people limiting the regular production of their goods to cover their families' needs. Any production that they may have had became very small, and they hoped that the Italians would not find it.

Little by little things started to get very strained not only with food, but with the relationship between the villagers and the enemy soldiers. The villagers all over our area started to organize and get ready to fight the enemy with whatever weapons they could find. There were clandestine meetings not only with our own villagers, but also with people from other villages in our area. Their objective was to disrupt the communications of the Italians, learn their every move, and in due time engage them in battle. The Italians had their own spies in the village. They were becoming aware if not of everything that was happening, at least of the organized undercurrent that was taking place. They learned about the meetings that were taking place in two houses. Fortunately, they did not know who the participants were. One of those houses belonged to my Grandfather Elias and the other to my father's godfather. The Italians ordered some village people to tear down those houses instead of setting them on fire. For some reason, they wanted to destroy those houses without affecting the neighboring homes. Those two homes became the first property casualties of war in Vrontama.

Several people who lived in Athens came to live with relatives in Vrontama to avoid the terrible events that followed in the big cities after the occupation. One woman who had a small store next to my grandfather's house hosted two young sisters from Athens who lived in a small apartment next to her store. These young ladies were quite pretty and worked as seamstresses for their food. I had to walk past their front door going to and from school. One time they stopped me and asked who I was. They were very nice and polite, so I told them who my parents were. All the time they were talking to me, they were staring at my eyes and told me that I had beautiful, black eyes. I was not used to anyone complimenting me in this way, and without saying anything, I ran as fast as I could to tell my mother. My mother asked me why I did not just say "Thank you" and walk home instead of running, but I had no answer. Coming from the big city, they were just trying to be nice to me. After that day, every time I walked to or from school, I hoped that the two sisters would not see me.

The resistance movement in our area started in Kosma when British commandos secretly parachuted into an area just outside the village. The British split up into two groups and went to the houses in the village to establish communications with their headquarters. Their objective was to help the Greek Resistance organize into a fighting force and supply it with arms to fight the enemy. My Grandfather Elias's house was one of the houses in which the British stayed. My Aunt Evgenia was their go-between within Kosma. All this was done in total secrecy, and information was given on a need-to-know basis. Only a handful of villagers and the leadership of the Resistance knew what was happening. Through radio communications the British had several air drops of weapons, ammunition, food and other supplies given to the Resistance in order to fight for the defeat of the common enemy. The resistance movement was organized with the help of the British. The Greeks did the fighting while the British helped with arms.

The first battle between the enemy and the Resistance took place just outside of Kosma on July 27, 1943 in which the Resistance had a major victory by killing most of the enemy including their commander. Only a handful escaped from the battle. This was the first organized engagement that took place in the Peloponnese up to that time, and it served as a morale booster for other resistance units in the area. They started to believe in their fighting capabilities. I was in Vrontama at the time, and looking toward Kosma I could see the smoke and hear the guns raging during that battle.

As if our family did not have enough problems, while in Kosma in the summer of 1941, I started having problems with the femur in my right leg. It started with a little pain. Within a month, my leg was swollen and I was in unbearable pain. Not having a doctor anywhere in the vicinity, my parents took me by horse to Vrontama and from there to Sparta to see Dr. Christos Karvounis who was a friend of my dad and a noted orthopedic physician. He had studied medicine in Germany. Dr. Karvounis had his own clinic on the main street of Sparta. As soon as he saw me, he diagnosed that I was suffering from osteomyelitis. He told my parents that if he did nothing, I would die within hours. And so, he operated immediately. The infection was so bad that as soon as the scalpel made the initial cut, the pus came out with such force that it sprayed the doctor and the operating room. We had no money to pay the doctor, so in gratitude to him for operating on me my mother cleaned every inch of the operating room, which had been contaminated with the pus from my leg. The infection was in the bone, so the doctor had to cut out a complete section of the bone. Naturally, I was told of all this a few days later. Antibiotics were nowhere to be found at that time which made my recovery slow and difficult.

After the operation, my dad went back to Vrontama where they had left my sister with my grandfather and Uncle John. I was sick with a high fever for weeks after the operation. My mother stayed with me in Sparta for almost two months, sleeping on a mat on the concrete floor next to my bed. There was a blackout in Sparta at that time. Mom had a small bowl with oil that she would light and hold next to my face to see if I were breathing. Because part of the bone in my femur was missing, Dr. Karvounis put my leg in traction to keep it straight until the bone could grow and reconnect. Since I was only seven years old at the time, the bone did grow into one piece, but because of the traction, the femur grew about ¾ of an inch longer than my left femur. This difference presented me with many problems as an adult.

The hunger in Sparta had started to take root. The clinic did not have any food for the patients, and even the doctor was facing hunger. My mother would get up at 4:00 A.M. to go stand for hours in whatever food line she could find just to get a handful of grapes. My dad would send us some fruits, vegetables and once in a while a chicken to keep us from starving. I shared my clinic room with a girl of my age whose mother was also staying with her. Everything that we received was shared with the doctor, his wife, the girl in my room, and her mother.

After two months, I still had a fever and was not getting any better. When my dad came to visit, my mother said she wanted to go home. She had not seen my five-year-old sister for months and was tired of the concrete floor and the blackout. My dad insisted that she stay. She said he could stay if he wanted to, but she wanted to take me home. The incision in my leg was not healing, and if I was going to die, I could die at home. Finally my dad agreed that we would all go home. When I left the clinic, I kissed the doctor's hand and thanked him for saving my life. My family was indebted to him for everything that he did for all of us, and we continued to send whatever food we were able to get to him. Unfortunately, in 1943 he was executed by the Germans with 117 other prominent citizens of Sparta.

My parents put me on a horse and started out for home. It was a long trip, about seven hours, for a little boy with an open wound and a fever. We stopped often by a river along the way so that they could try to lower my temperature. After we got home, a distant cousin of my mother who lived in the nearby village of Geraki came to visit. She was known for her herbal and natural remedies. When she returned to her village, she made a salve out of some plants and sent it to my mother to put on my incision. After a while, little pieces of bone started coming out of the hole. Eventually, it healed and my fever went away. This healing, however, was temporary, and I was to have more attacks of osteomyelitis in my teens and twenties. Little did I know when I was a young boy that this disease would ultimately bring me to America and set me on a journey that I never could have imagined.

The German Occupation

As the occupation continued and our freedom was restricted with more raids on our homes, so did the determination of the people to oppose the enemy in every way they could. By early 1943, the Germans started to take a more active part in the occupation of Greece, at least in the southern part, and started to push their Italian allies into getting tougher with the Greek population. The Germans were now becoming the main occupation force in all the surrounding areas. They would stay in town for a few days, and after they took all the food supplies they could get, they would leave only to come back a few days later for more supplies and to let the developing Resistance know that they were being watched.

As they were leaving town after one of the raids, they took one of our horses and a mule from the aloni where they were grazing. We did not see those animals until the end of the war when we saw them coming to town by themselves and heading home to my grandfather's house. Both animals were skin and bones, but everyone in the family was happy to see them. My Uncle John and my dad did everything they could to make them healthy again by giving them plenty of water and hay to eat. After a few days we found them dead in one of our fields where we usually took them for grazing. That was a sad day for our entire family.

Members of the Gestapo fluent in Greek were always present at every raid. They had established a network of domestic spies within the village's population, people who were willing to spy and give information to the enemy in order to get even with people that they may have had disagreements with in the past. There were only a handful of people who were involved in this treasonous behavior. My father and a few other prominent men had become targets of the Germans every time they came to town.

During the entire occupation, there was always someone in the bell tower of our church on the lookout for Germans. The bell tower was high enough to spot the German columns when they were miles away. During the occupation, the church bells were rung only when the Germans were observed coming to our village. When people heard the church bells, especially the leaders of the village such as my dad, they would come home, load the horses with blankets, food and other things that we needed, and we would run out of the village quickly. Many times we were awakened in the middle of the night and walked in total darkness to an unknown destination. Our goal was to get out of the village and go somewhere where we could not be seen by the enemy. When my father thought we had enough distance between us and the Germans, we unloaded the animals, put some blankets on the ground and fell asleep, only to wake up with the sun and try to determine our location. Not having any kind of light available, we were not always aware of the type of terrain we slept on. A few times, we found ourselves sleeping on ant nests, and other times we had scorpions and a snake for company in the morning.

The German raids were not always carried out at night. One time, in order to catch the village by surprise, a German column of trucks and tanks was seen heading for our village after church services, and church bells rang to warn the people of their arrival. My entire family had gone to church that Sunday morning. We had just come home and were ready to eat a soup that my mother had prepared when we heard the bells, which was the signal for my family to leave. My father and Uncle John got our two horses loaded with the usual supplies, and we all got ready to leave. My mother put the soup back in the pot, sealed it as well as she could, put it on top of the horse and we all rushed to get out of town. We were all hungry, so we stopped where we thought we would be safe, took the pot with the soup down from the horse, spread out a blanket and had just started eating when people coming behind us told us that the Germans were coming right behind them. We put the pot of soup back on the horse, grabbed the blanket and started running again. When we reached the top of the next hill, we saw the Germans at the place we had just left. They fired their machine guns at us, but by then we were over the hill and they missed us. We traveled for what seemed a very long time and ended up at a shack at my Grandfather Elias' vineyard. Everyone was hungry and tired of running. My mother said she did not care if the Germans were coming anymore; we were going to sit and eat. And that is what we did.

It was Tuesday of Holy Week when the enemy was seen coming to our village from the southwest, headed toward the Evrotas River. They were accompanied by several armored vehicles and other small artillery pieces. Holy Week is very important in the Orthodox Church. The local Resistance decided to defend the village at least until after Easter. They set the line of defense on our aloni, which is the highest point of the village looking down and across the river. There were around fifty fighters, and their weapons were only a few machine guns and rifles. Children of my age were asked to unpack the ammunition behind the lines and carry it to the men on the front line. And so it was. When the fighting started, our job was to make sure that the men on the front lines had ammunition for their weapons. The Germans were held on the other side of the river until dark, and then they started firing their artillery and mortars toward us. We saw two mortar shells explode on the side of our church leaving two holes in it. The commander of the defenders, after seeing that they were no match for the enemy's strength, told his troops to retreat from their positions and save their ammunition to fight another day. When I went home, I got the usual scolding from my mother for having participated in the fighting. My father arrived soon with the horses, and the entire family got out of town heading away from the enemy. We did not know the reason, but the Germans stayed in town for only a few hours and then left the village heading toward the Parnonas Mountain. Why did they leave so early? No one knew. Some people said that the German commander must have been a Christian and decided to move his troops out and let us celebrate Easter in peace. Whatever the reason was, the people were happy to be able to celebrate the Lord's Resurrection in peace.

Greek money did not have any value during the occupation. But even if it had value, there was nothing available to buy. The pair of shoes that I had right before the war I wore until the end of the war. My father cut the top front cover of the shoes and my toes stuck out. When the soles of the shoes wore out, he took them to a prewar shoemaker in town who added a sole made from old tires left behind by the enemy. I was not the exception to not having shoes; most of the children and adults in the village were in the same boat. Many adults did not even have shoes at all. They wore sandals made out of wood to avoid walking barefoot on the rough terrain of the village and to work in their fields. If there was any commerce in Vrontama, it was done with barter. If someone needed milk, they would pay with flour, potatoes, lentils or beans, etc. Most of the time these exchanges were done in secrecy because the enemy would take whatever was bartered for their own use.

One morning in the spring of 1943, we woke up and saw all the Italians that were the everyday occupation force standing in a circle in the village square with their hands up in the air and their weapons in the middle. One can imagine the curiosity that this situation ignited. People walked to the square, and the Italians made it known that the war was over for them and that they did not want to fight any longer. The antartes (resistance fighters) came to town. They took the weapons from the Italians and their boots for their own use and asked the people who could afford to feed another mouth to take an Italian soldier to their house. My dad asked one of the officers to come to our house. His official name was Domenick Teggi, and we called him "Kyriako," the Greek version of Domenick. Kyriako was in his mid-twenties, an educated and well-mannered man. He became a regular member of our family. He insisted on going out in the fields and working like any other member of the family. When we had to get out of the village to avoid the German raids, Kyriako was the first to help with the horses, the supplies and me and my sister to get ready for departure. The Italians had become the enemy of the Germans, and if they got caught, they were executed immediately. Kyriako went wherever we went, and many times he would help the antartes with information about the Germans.

In April 1943, my Grandfather Elias passed away after a long bout with throat cancer. I was playing with other children on the church grounds on that day when my mother sent someone to tell me that my grandfather had died. I immediately went inside the church and climbed the stairs to the tower in order to ring the bells and tell everyone that there was a death in the village. Needless to say, when I reached the top of the tower, I was stopped from ringing the bells because that was the signal that the Germans were coming.

The German raids started to come more frequently, and many times they came to town without being noticed by the lookout people in the church's bell tower. They would come on foot in the dark of night and have their vehicles, trucks, tanks and motorcycles driven into town later. We did not always have time to leave, and my mother would take us to someone else's house to stay until the Germans left town. My father, Uncle John and Kyriako would find a way to get out of town and hide in the fields as best they could. One time when they were hiding in a cave and the Germans were walking around outside, Kyriako was bitten by a scorpion. Scorpion bites are very painful. My dad and uncle quickly pushed his head in the dirt so that the Germans would not hear him cry out.

On July 12, 1944 the Germans came to Vrontama undetected, but my father, Uncle John and Kyriako were able to leave and narrowly avoided capture by the enemy. My mother took me and my sister to my grandfather's house and stayed there for a few nights. Two days later, on my tenth birthday, when we woke up in the morning, we saw clouds of smoke coming from the direction of our house and the house of a leader of the Resistance. As our house was burning to the ground, a Greek-speaking Gestapo stood on the balcony yelling for my dad to come and save his house. I went toward the house to see what was happening and tried to jump over the fence to get something that at the time was important to me. A soldier yelled at me to stop. I started to run away when I heard gun shots behind me. Fortunately, either he was not a good shot or he just wanted to scare me. Of the few shots that were fired toward me, one barely hit my upper right arm. I felt nothing until my mother noticed that there was blood running down my right hand. She yelled at me for a while, and then she washed my arm with homemade alcohol and bandaged it. In a few days, I was as good as new. I still have the scar on my arm.

The next day the Germans came to my grandfather's house to ask my mother where my father was. Not knowing where he was, she told them that she did not know. Even if she had known, her answer would have been the same. One of the Germans raised his rifle and began hitting my mother on the back with the rifle butt. I ran to the soldier and started to kick him to distract him from my mother. He turned around and slapped me on the head, and I fell on the ground. He then walked away and left my mother and me alone. My mother suffered back pain from that beating for the rest of her life.

In the early fall of 1944, the word got out that the Germans were ready to raid our village with many troops and stay for longer than usual. They considered the area as one of the hotbeds of resistance activity and wanted to eliminate it. The antartes passed the word around of what was coming and most of the people involved in any resistance activity were able to get out of town. Our family was no exception. We went to a location about ten kilometers southeast of Vrontama where the terrain was so mountainous that the Germans would not dare to come with any of their tanks or even motorcycles. We ended up on the east part of the mountain, away from the village in a large cave that was used by a shepherd for his goats. Another thirty people came along to share that cave with us.

The women had brought with them whatever food supplies they could find, mostly beans for soup. No one, however, thought to bring utensils or large bowls to use for eating. Our water supply was the Evrotas River which was about 200 yards below the cave. In order to get the water, we had to climb down on the side of the mountain to fill up some pottery containers with water and bring them up to the cave for everyone to drink. Everyone was taking their turn for this task. When my cousin Georgia was on her way up the mountain, she hit the container on a rock and broke it into two pieces, each of them resembling a large soup bowl. When my mother saw this, she thought of it as an opportunity to use the two pieces as platters for serving the bean soup. Since we had only two or three spoons, we sat in a large circle and each of us took his or her turn for a spoonful of beans and then passed the spoon to the next person for their turn. This went on until all the soup was gone. During the day, the men took turns going to the top of the mountain to observe any possible movement of the Germans toward our location. No enemy was ever seen. We were safe.

During our stay in the cave, I found a very narrow path at the edge of the mountain which led to the other side of the mountain. It was very risky for me to go to the other side because if I had fallen, my next stop would have been about 100 meters into the river. I did this without telling my mother and went to the other side to meet the shepherds who owned the goats. I made friends with them, and every time I went there they gave me goat's milk to drink. Eventually my mother caught on to this activity, but after I told her that the shepherds were giving me milk, she gave me her blessing to continue going there.

The nights were very cold in the cave, and many of the goats would come from the hillsides and sleep on the high sides of the cave with us. During the night, the goats dropped their droppings which in many cases would fall on our faces and for those who snored, in their mouth. We stayed in that cave for about twelve days, and I still remember so many details about our stay there. Everyone got along well with each other. When the guards on the top of the hill saw that the Germans were leaving town, we waited for a day, and then we all returned home.

Since our house had been burned, we had moved to a house on the village square. Every time we left the village to avoid the German raids, we came back to find the house in shambles. While the soldiers stayed on the second floor, they put their horses and mules on the ground floor. The animals would do their poop inside the house, and the soldiers would break whatever they found on the top floor. This was repeated every time we came back after an enemy raid. My mother and father and we children would spend at least two days making the house livable again.

In 1944, we anticipated a German raid in our village with many troops. The rumor was that they were going to burn every house in Vrontama because of the village's support of the antartes. When people heard about this, they started making preparations on how to save some of the things that they would need after their house was burned. My Grandfather George's house had a cement balcony over the front entrance of the house which had empty space under it. We stored most of the food supplies that we had along with some clothes and blankets under the balcony, and then the adults built a solid wall around as a support of the balcony. The wall was painted and everyone hoped for the best. As it turned out, the Germans did come to town but left in a hurry going north, and thus Vrontama was saved. The reason for leaving quickly was that they had orders to move north and engage the Allies in Western Europe.

The family that lived across the street from my grandfather's house had a radio. A radio at that time was contraband, but somehow they brought it from Athens and had it before the war. Since we did not have electricity in the village, someone had to turn a small generator by hand for the radio to work. Every night most of the people in the village congregated in front of my grandfather's house to listen to the BBC news that was broadcasted in Greek. When the enemy was not in town, that radio kept us informed on what was happening on the various fronts of the war. I still remember the exultation of everyone when we heard of the Allied invasion of France and the victories that followed till the end of the war.

School during the Occupation

The school was up the street from my Grandfather George's house, next to our church. It had only two rooms, so some grades had to attend classes together in the morning and the rest in the afternoon. Needless to say, the school was very cold in the winter months during which the temperature would drop below freezing. The children were asked to bring one good piece of wood everyday for the potbelly stoves that were providing the heat in each classroom. We still had to wear our heavy clothing even though we had a stove. It was helpful, but not enough to keep us warm.

Most of the time, we had two teachers in the school. One of them was married to my father's cousin. Her husband was the first person in Vrontama to die when he was shot by thieves while protecting the potatoes he had planted. She was the toughest teacher in the eyes of all of us children. She was a very strict disciplinarian. If she caught us at mischievous activity, it meant corporal punishment with us providing the weapon. We were told to go outside, find a good stick from a nearby olive tree and bring it to her. She used that stick to hit us on the legs in front of the whole class. The more we cried, the longer the punishment lasted. When it was over, we had to apologize for what we had done and go to our seat. The teacher was always right as far as our parents were concerned. Therefore, it was not to our advantage to tell our parents of the punishment we received. The other teacher was a man who was very mild in our punishment and in temperament. The teachers were very sympathetic to the national Resistance and were also in danger of losing their lives if caught by the Germans. Naturally, there was no school during the German raids. When I think about it now that I am in my seventies, I do not know how in the world we learned what we did in that chaotic atmosphere. Some of my peers from that time have become doctors, teachers and good business people who have contributed a great deal to society. There were others who because of the war and their parents' indifference have contributed very little besides caring for their own families. Some of them even grew up to despise those who had made something of themselves.

Local Civil Authorities during the Occupation

Although the village was occupied most of the time by the enemy, the elders organized in such a manner that even when the enemy was there, there was multi-faceted underground work always going on. One of the first organizations was the Hellenic Liberation Front (EAM). This became the political arm of the Resistance, offering their assistance to the antartes who were directly fighting the enemy. My father had become the head of this organization, which made him a target for the enemy. There were women's organizations whose function was to collect blankets, food, etc., and even sew uniforms for the antartes. Young people between the ages of sixteen to twenty-one had their own organization, and their job was to observe the enemy and pass on intelligence information to EAM that after verification would in turn be passed on to the antartes.

When the war came to us, all civil authorities were dismantled. There were situations that had to be resolved: conflicts between Vrontama citizens that were leading to animosity and actual thefts from other people's farms and their gardens. There were cases where an owner of an olive grove would harvest the olives on his own property and also some of the olives from his neighbor's property. Naturally this created conflicts between friends and neighbors which resulted in discord in the entire village. At times, people would tell lies about each other to the enemy. This was not helping the cohesiveness that was needed within the resistance effort. The elders decided to organize a civil court to resolve such issues and appointed levelheaded citizens to serve as judges. My father was one of the judges for a while. Needless to say that when things did not go the way of some who had been brought to court, they blamed the judges, and in many cases the judges became their targets in the civil war that followed the occupation. Some women were brought to court for fraternizing with the enemy, and the court always punished them by cutting off their hair.

The initial stage for famine was set. Many people who could not hide their food from the enemy started to suffer from hunger and were begging for food from their friends and relatives who also were facing the same problems. The truth is that my family did not experience much hunger. It did not mean that we had all the food that we needed, but compared to other families, we were somewhat better off. My father, foreseeing the war coming, managed to hide some wheat, flour, olive oil and edible olives in places that the enemy would not look. My mother would share small portions of what we had with everyone who came to the door looking for food even if she had to take it away from our family.

The hunger was getting worse not only in our village, but everywhere in Greece and especially in Athens. We were getting reports that people in Athens were experiencing famine of biblical proportions. People were falling in the streets and dying from hunger without anyone even turning their heads. Death was everywhere people turned. City trucks would come around twice a day, and men would pick up the bodies, throw them on the trucks, and bury them in mass graves. Families with children were putting their children on trucks, buses or any other type of transportation they could find and sending them anywhere someone could take them in and give them food so that they could live. The parents did not even know where their own children were going. They only knew that if they stayed with them in the city they would die. Their children's best chance for survival was for them to be anywhere but in Athens.

One day six or seven children were brought to our village. Eleni was one of those children. We did not know until later how or from where she came to Vrontama with the other children. Eleni was a year older than my sister, and my mom and dad thought that we could provide a reasonable home for her for the duration of the war. And so, they brought her home to live with us as our sister. She stayed with us for almost two years. A first cousin of my mother from Kosma sent her youngest son to live with us after their house was burned along with the rest of the village.

We all got along very well, and we shared the good times and the bad together. My mom, however, had a huge responsibility to take care of all of us. Everyone ate whatever was available for my mom to prepare. We always said our prayers as expected, whether we liked the food or not. My favorite food during the occupation was lentils with homemade noodles that my mother would make whenever we had flour. This and beans were the main meals that we had several times a week. The butchers in town were mostly out of business because animals were not available to be slaughtered. Most of the time we had a goat for the milk it gave us, and once a year she was pregnant. When the little goats matured, their meat found a place on our dinner table. This accounted for the few times we ate meat during the occupation. Once in a while my father would bring a few pigeons that were given to him by an older man who wanted my father to check his blood pressure. This man lived across the street from my grandfather's house and had a small tower next to his home where he raised pigeons. We always hoped that he would ask my dad to visit him so that he would give him more pigeons. My mother cleaned the pigeons and cooked them for all of us to eat. That was a delicacy that we always looked forward to having on the table.

Pumpkins were another source of food for us. My parents devoted a small part of the field by the river to growing pumpkins. I always looked forward to the season when the pumpkins were ready for harvest. My mom would cut the pumpkin in two halves and give a spoon to each of us to scrape the inside of each half. Then she would spread the chopped pumpkin on a baking pan on top of homemade dough leaves. After she added rice and raisins, she would cover the whole thing with more dough leaves and put it in the oven outside of the house. When it finished baking, mom would put some honey on top, and when it cooled off, it was our dinner for the day. We children loved this pumpkin dinner, and when the adults were not looking we took the liberty of eating some before dinner. That did not please my mother very much, but we were not punished unless we had company and did not have enough food for everybody. In that case, we were not allowed to have pumpkin pie. We had to eat whatever was left from the previous day.

The Liberation

Starting in late 1944, the German raids had become fewer and fewer, and by the middle of the next year the raids had stopped. The Germans were losing the war on all fronts, and the Allies started their march for the final blow to Nazi Germany. The Germans were coming through Vrontama only to move on toward the northern part of Greece and then toward Germany to defend it from the Allies. During the retreat they were engaged in battle with units of the Resistance which eventually benefited the Allies' march to Germany.

The liberation was anticipated in our village because of the news heard on the secret radio. All the villages in our area and Sparta were liberated about two months before the liberation of Athens. People from the villages, including Vrontama, went to Sparta and celebrated their freedom for days, singing songs of the Resistance in the streets of Sparta. Thousands of people marched in the streets, even some of the British soldiers who were there. I was in the fourth grade at the time. Our teachers led us in the singing of our national anthem and told us all to go to our church next to the school and light a candle to thank God for our freedom.

While my family and I rejoiced in the freedom that came to us with liberation from the enemy, it also brought some sadness, especially when we had to say goodbye to the people who had spent the occupation with us. First, Kyriako left and returned to Italy. I can never forget the emotional goodbye with Kyriako. He knelt before my parents, and with tears in his eyes kissed their hands and thanked them for everything they had done for him. We were all in tears as he hugged me and my sister goodbye and left for home after living with us for over two years. We thought of him as a true member of our family, and when he left, it was like one of us had left the family never to return again. Kyriako sent my parents letters after he got home thanking them for saving his life. He sent us pictures of himself and later with his wife when he got married.

The other loss that we children felt was that of the young girl, Eleni, who had also stayed with us during the war. Her parents found out where she was and came to Vrontama to take her back home to Athens. That was another emotional goodbye, especially for both sets of parents. They did not know how to thank us enough for saving their daughter from the terrible famine that took place in Athens. I do not recall seeing Eleni again after she left us, but I think that my father kept in communication with her father.

The Katsicopoulos family members were American citizens, and when the war ended, they were notified by the American Embassy that they could return home to Dayton, Ohio where Mr. Katsicopoulos lived. One day in April 1946 a truck pulled up in front of my grandfather's house to carry the family to Athens from where they would go to America. That was a very sad day, especially for me who thought of George as a big brother. It was a school day, but I wanted to see the Katsicopoulos family leave because I thought that I would never see them again. After the truck left, I stayed at my grandfather's front door crying and waiving goodbye even when I was not able to see them.

This created another problem for me. I was supposed to be in school that day, and I knew that I would be disciplined by my teacher, who always believed in corporal punishment. I wanted to avoid that, so I sat down and wrote a note to the teacher on behalf of my father saying, "My son George was sick yesterday and that is the reason he was not in school." When she read the note, she knew that the handwriting was not my father's. I was surprised when she confronted me telling me that I had lied to her, and I admitted that I had written the note myself. She did not punish me, but she told me that she was going to give the note to my father. That day had become another bad day for me. How was I going to explain this to my father when he got home?

My teacher went to see my father at the store and gave him the note along with the whole story that I had told her. I had to tell my father what really had happened, and he patiently listened to every word that I said. When I finished, he slapped the top of my hands several times and told me that I was being punished not for skipping school the day before, but for lying to my teacher on his behalf. He understood my emotional state when George left Vrontama, but he told me that if he ever caught me lying again, he would throw me out of the house. I had to apologize to my dad, my mother, my Uncle John, my grandfather, my teacher and my whole class the next day.

With the end of the war and the Atlantic opening up for commercial traffic again, our American relatives started to send us care packages with clothes, shoes and other items that we all needed, especially since our house and everything we owned had been burned by the Germans. When the packages arrived, my parents kept what we could use and distributed the rest of the items to other people in the village who could use them. Most of the packages that we received were sent to us by my mother's sister, Marigo Pappas, and my father's brother, George Manos. My mother's brother Tony Lambros from Australia sent several packages with new shoes to the village of Kosma. The shoes were to be distributed to the school children. I was given a pair of those shoes, and I finally threw away the shoes that I had worn for several years with the tops cut off for my growing feet.

Although my Grandfather Elias' house in Kosma had been burned by the Germans, my parents still wanted me and my sister to stay in Kosma with my Aunt Evgenia who was always there during the summer months. The only things that survived the fire were the four walls and the concrete balcony in front of the house. The balcony, which measured approximately seven feet by ten feet, became our home for the first summer after the occupation. That was where we slept, where we sat in the cool evenings, and where we kept all our possessions. Fortunately, the front wall of the house was still standing, and the balcony's metal cover provided cover from rain and the sun. Two of the other three sides were protected with wooden boards that we put up while the entrance at the top of the slate steps leading to the balcony was always open. Everyone in the village found themselves in the same situation. We all trusted each other in the village because we were all in the same boat trying to survive and to salvage anything that we could. The outhouse on the side of the house and a small cooking area survived the fire and became useful for us and even for some of our neighbors. In spite of those living conditions, my sister and I coped quite well with everything that summer. At least we were not being chased in the mountains by the enemy.

Within a short time after war, we were notified that my father's brother from America had sent us a horse and a mule. My father had to go to Sparta to pick them up and bring them home. The horse was a red mare and a real beauty, and the mule was brown. I loved riding the horse and always looked forward to taking it for a ride to the village's water wells and for other chores. And so the horses that we had lost were replaced by those two wonderful animals that came from America. We were once again able to use them for plowing the fields, transportation and for other work associated with farming. Unfortunately, within a year we had to leave our village to save our lives, and the two animals were left with our relatives.

As strange as it might seem today, in spite of the raids by the enemy and the hardships my family and I went through during the war, we also had a certain amount of peace within us. Most of the people in the village were united in fighting the enemy and had set aside personal or family differences. Unfortunately, all that came to an end after the enemy left and the civil war started.

The Civil War

After the liberation, bad politics by Greek politicians, the British, and some members of the Resistance during the occupation resulted in a chaotic situation. The command of the Resistance was tricked by both British and Greek politicians into giving up their arms, while militias that had cooperated with the enemy were allowed to keep theirs and authorized to turn against those who had fought the enemy during the occupation. The people who had given everything that they had for the cause of freedom during the Italian and German occupations now found themselves on the defensive against the very same people who had cooperated with the enemy.

It was rumored that in one of the meetings that Winston Churchill had with members of the Greek government after the war, he directed them to capture, imprison and if necessary kill all the leaders of the wartime Resistance. The underlying reason for this was that in northern Greece, former resistance fighters were influenced and supported by the Iron Curtain countries. When the Greek army was once again established after the war, it fought in northern Greece against the Communist-supported rebels who were trying to takeover Greece and expand the Communist influence. With American aid, the Communists failed in their goal, and when the civil war was over in 1949, Greece remained a free country.

There was another type of civil war going on in the southern part of the Peloponnese. The Greek army concentrated its efforts on fighting in the north. This gave the opportunity for several militias to surface who took it upon themselves to kill anyone who had participated in the resistance movement during the occupation under the pretence that they were all Communists.

And so, the worst nightmare of our village and other villages in the area started. Those militia thugs started to court the people in the village who were sympathetic to the enemy during the occupation and who had actually committed acts of treason. Some of them had appeared in the makeshift court during the occupation and were penalized for their acts. None of them had been sentenced to death. Their punishment was the loss of food items, such as olive oil, wheat, etc. Those few men combined their efforts with the outlaw militias to destroy the leaders of the village and label them as Communists. At that time, once someone was labeled as a Communist, whether they were Communists or not, they became a target for execution.

My father was not a Communist, but a true patriot who loved his country and his village more than himself. The Communist label, however, was applied to him along with the other prominent people of Vrontama. He became a target for execution. If caught, those labeled as Communists were executed almost immediately, and their heads were taken to Sparta so the executioners could collect their bounty.

I can think of no one from Vrontama who was a Communist. The people who had fought with the Resistance were true patriots and men of great honor and courage who gave their all to fight the enemy and assist the Allies in the final defeat of the Axis. The British who had encouraged, helped and supported the Resistance during the war turned against them at the end of the occupation and gave orders to capture and execute the people who had helped them during the war. My father could not forget this betrayal and despised the British until the end of his life.

At the beginning of this nightmare, we lived in a house right on the village square. The militias would bring prisoners from other villages to Vrontama and keep them locked up in a building across the square from where we lived. The prisoners brought to the building across the square were tortured day and night, and their screams and cries for mercy were heard by the entire village, especially at night. When the sounds of torture stopped, we knew that the prisoners had been taken out and executed outside the village. I will never forget the terror that we children felt. We could not even walk outside of our house and go to my grandfather's house up the street without feeling terrified that we would be stopped and questioned. I realized that I was losing the world that I had known up to that point. I was only eleven years old, but I knew that our village was no longer a friendly place. Now I had to be careful about what I said to and about people that I had known all my life. Although my world had changed, I thought that after a while things would go back as they had been. But they never did.

In the middle of one night, someone knocked on our door and asked us if he could hide in our house until he was able to escape from Vrontama and go to Sparta or Athens. He was one of the commanders of the Resistance from another village and was marked for death by the militias. He was not a stranger to us because during the occupation my father had brought him to our house several times. He came to our house for two reasons: one, he knew that we would not betray him, and two, no one would think that we would hide someone so close to where the prisoners were being held and tortured. He stayed with us for three days, and with help from other people, he dressed as a woman, left in the darkness of night and eventually went to Athens. The next time we saw him was in Athens at a coffeehouse named "Neon."

The sounds of torture had become so bad that we could not take it any more. We moved to my Aunt Marigo's house in which we had lived before my parents bought the house from the Lyskas family in 1939. That house, as I mentioned before, was burned by the Germans.

With help from the militias, those who had been traitors during the war took over the reins of our village's town council. The six village council members met on March 28, 1946 in secrecy with the goal to discredit fifty outstanding citizens with their American relatives. Every one of these fifty people was accused of unspeakable crimes that never happened and was labeled a Communist. A three-page letter was written full of false accusations and hate and was sent to all the Americans for whom they had an address. The letter said that all of these men were to be eliminated in order for the village to become peaceful and for the Americans to stop sending any kind of help to their families.

After the war, the Americans started to send money and clothes to their relatives in order to help them until they were able to get on their feet. The letter stated that the Americans should stop helping these fifty families immediately because they were not worthy of their assistance. I have a copy of this letter and have read it many times trying to find some justification for such action. I was eleven years old at the time, and I still remember the names and faces of most of the people in that letter.

While only a few people in our village died in battle against the enemy during the war, during the period between 1946 and 1949, ninety-four people died in Vrontama alone from the so-called militias with the cooperation of Vrontama traitors. Many of the killings were carried out by these local traitors. The inhumane treatment of the so-called prisoners was not enough. After we safely arrived in Athens in the summer of 1946, we were informed that the most notorious leader of the militias captured a member of the Resistance from another village and brought him to the square in Vrontama for execution. For his own amusement, he gave an ax to a villager and told him to cut off the prisoner's head with it. When the villager refused to do it, he pointed a gun at his head and told him that if he did not do it, he was going to shoot him. The man, thinking of his family, decapitated the man whom he did not even know. That person was never the same after that; he went crazy thinking of what he had done and died a year later. Years after 1949, a man who had fully co-operated with the militias and had been responsible for many of the deaths that took place during the civil war regained his conscience to the point that he committed suicide by jumping in one of the village wells and drowning.

During one of the raids by the militia, my father was captured and taken away. The head of the militia was a young man whose sister had been in the same clinic room with me when I had my first operation and with whom my mother had shared our food. My mother saved that man's sister and his mother from starvation, and he saved my father from being tortured. My father was taken to a prison in Sparta to stand trial on a trumped-up charge of killing someone in another village.

In the meantime, the osteomyelitis in my right leg flared up again, and it became obvious that I would have to see a doctor. My father was in a prison in Sparta waiting for his trial. My mother took me to Sparta on a horse and went to see my dad who was still in prison to tell him about my ailment. My dad talked to the authorities and asked them to allow him to go outside and find some kind of transportation for me and my mom to go to Tripoli to see a good physician. After a few hours, my dad made arrangements with a military truck driver to allow me and my mother to get in the back of the truck that was headed for Tripoli. I can never forget the pain that I experienced in my leg while I waited for my turn to go to the operating table. The pain was so severe that I was begging my mother to take me to the doctor to give me something to relieve the pain. A few days later, I had the operation, and in a week I was released and returned to Vrontama. As it turned out, that was not the end of my medical problems.

After a few months my dad was found innocent because witnesses placed him in Sparta when the crime had been committed in the village.

Escape from Vrontama

Vrontama had become a village under siege. The roads to and from Vrontama were closed, and in order to come in or out, you had to have someone in authority in the village give you permission. Men were caught and tortured in the village square before they were taken away and executed.

My father left Vrontama and went to Kosma where things were somewhat less dangerous. My mother decided to leave Vrontama and go stay in Kosma until my dad decided on what to do next. But in order to leave town, we had to have the written permission of the so-called president of the council. I remember when my mother and I went to this person's home to ask for permission to leave. He told us that if we told him where my father was, he would let us leave. I am not sure whether my mom knew where my dad was or not. In any case, she told him that she did not know. Then she pleaded with him to let us go. After he refused, she asked for me and my sister to be allowed to leave by ourselves while my mother stayed in Vrontama. He decided to allow me and my sister to leave the following morning. We contacted my cousin Georgia who also had permission to leave Vrontama with us to bring her donkey to carry any supplies that we were able to bring with us.

I went to see my grandfather who had broken his hip at the beginning of the war and could only walk with crutches. I said goodbye to him, and with tears running down my face, I asked for his blessing and forgiveness for anything that I may have done to disappoint him. We both cried for a while and he told me to go with God and that we would see each other after the storm. Little did I know that this was the last time I would see my grandfather. My sister, my cousin Georgia and I left after midnight for Kosma, a six-hour trip by foot. As we walked out of the village, I continued to look back at the place where I had enjoyed living all my life. I just could not believe that I was leaving the village that I loved so much with the fear that I would not be coming back soon. I kept hoping that after things got better, my family would again reunite in Vrontama and our life would return to normal. My wish, however, would never come true. By the time the sun came up, we were at my Grandfather Elias' house in Kosma where Aunt Evgenia was waiting for us.

A month after I left Vrontama, the worst period started everywhere including in Kosma. One morning while everyone was still asleep, the militias from Mani (the southern-most area of Lakonia) came to Vrontama and surrounded our village letting no one leave for any reason. They went house to house and forced everyone to go to the village square for a meeting. People who were hiding or did not want to go were forced and some were even beaten. These outlaws, fully armed and with belts of ammunition around their shoulders, started to read the names of the men that they wanted. My mother was in Vrontama and present during this ordeal. They read over forty names. Two of them were the names of my father and Uncle John who had successfully escaped by hiding in a neighbor's storage of hay. Fortunately, neither of them was present. They forced my mother to take them to the house, and they searched everywhere to find them. They did not find them and let my mother go. Any of the men there whose names were called were arrested and made to walk toward the village of Grammoussa, about ten kilometers south of Vrontama. It was the middle of August when the heat of the sun is unbearable. Four of those men were executed on the way to Grammousa and the rest were marched to Skala. The killings eventually claimed ninety-four innocent lives in our village between 1946 and 1949. Somehow my mother found a way to come to Kosma a few days after this purge and joined my dad, me and my sister. Unfortunately, we, as a family, were not safe even in Kosma.

Escape from Kosma

During my first month in Kosma, I enjoyed the usual activities that I always did with my Kosma friends every summer. One of my responsibilities before I went to play was to make sure that there was plenty of water in the house. No one had running water in the village. So, I had to go to the fountains at the village square with a ten gallon bucket, fill it with water, and bring it home. It was not as easy as it sounds to bring that bucket of water home. Not only was it heavy, but also on the way home some of the water would splash out and I would have to make two trips to the fountains.

About a month later my mother and father came to Kosma, and once again I felt the child's security of being with my parents. I thought that by the end of the summer of 1946 things would be better, we would return home to Vrontama, and I would start going to high school in either Geraki or Sparta. That was never to happen.

My father felt somewhat safe in Kosma, as we all did, because up to that time the militias had not come to Kosma. My father went freely to the village square and had refreshments with his friends, one of whom was the village policeman. One afternoon he left a group of his friends in the square and went to see a relative. Within minutes after he left, those militias accompanied by some men from our village encircled the entire square and went directly to the table where my father had just been sitting. Not finding him there, they started looking for him in the narrow streets leading to the houses on the hill. Fortunately, a relative saw my father, who was not aware of the Kosma siege, and helped him escape from one house to another until the next day.

Not being able to find my father anywhere, they came to my grandfather's house where the rest of us were staying. Along with the militia men, there were two men from Vrontama. They rushed into the house, turned the beds and other furniture upside down, and started to interrogate all of us about the whereabouts of my father. We knew that if they found him he would be executed. Actually, none of us knew where my father was; even if we had known, we would never have told them. It was obvious that my father was a wanted man, and it was only a matter of time before he would be killed if he stayed around Kosma or Vrontama. The day after that raid, my mother received word from my father saying that he wanted to leave the village and go to Sparta and from there to Athens. My Aunt Evgenia's husband, who was also in Kosma at that time and had received threats on his life from the same group of criminals, decided to join my father in escaping to Athens. Uncle Nick had two brothers in Athens who were high-ranking police officials. If their escape to Athens was successful, they knew that they would be safe there.

In the meantime, the rest of us stayed in Kosma while my mother tried to decide on our next move. Going in and out of the village had become very difficult. All the roads were heavily guarded by the militias who were not letting anyone through without a permit. The word got out that the militias had moved toward Vrontama and had left the roadblocks that they had established around Kosma. My Aunt Evgenia and my mother saw this as an opportunity for at least some of us to leave and go to Leonidion, a large city about thirty-five kilometers east of Kosma, and from there take a boat to Athens. The decision was made that Aunt Evgenia would take me, my sister and my cousin Georgia with her to Athens, and then return to Kosma to eventually bring my mother and my cousin Popi to Athens. Aunt Evgenia felt somewhat safe doing this because of her brothers-in-law's positions in the Athens police. And so, under the cover of darkness and with the help of the horse driver next door and his horses, we said our goodbyes to my mother and left for Leonidion. Little did I know that I was saying goodbye to the life that I had loved as a child and entering into a totally different adventure and phase of my life.

The road to Leonidion was made up of small, narrow paths that the horses were barely able to negotiate. We had to come down some very steep mountainous terrain. I was holding on to the saddle of my horse for dear life while the horse driver tried to tell us stories to take our minds away from the road. We finally arrived at Leonidion and went directly to a distant relative's house to wait for the boat that would take us to Athens during the night. The word came that the militias had come to Leonidion looking for people that were from Kosma. We were asked to go to the basement of the house and not come up until it was time to leave for the boat. Finally when night came, we were helped to go to the boat dock and get on the boat. That was the first time that I saw a boat much less got on one. To say that I was a little scared is an understatement.

The boat was around forty to fifty feet long, and all the passengers had to sit on benches that were placed around the deck. It was not a passenger boat; it must have been a fishing boat, but no one cared. It was our ticket to a terror-free life. I did not sleep all night. I was constantly looking over the side of the boat to see if there were any fish in the sea. I could not see anything until morning when I did see several dolphins swimming next to us. I remember how excited I was to see the dolphins. I had never seen one except in a picture in a textbook. We finally arrived in Pireaus, the port city of Athens, where my father and Uncle Nick were waiting for us.

Even after we left our villages, the hate against my family continued. I had a dog that my parents had given me while in Vrontama, and in our rush to survive, my dog was left behind in my grandfather's house. One of the militia leaders saw my dog in front of my grandfather's house and asked a neighbor who was the dog's owner. When he was told that the dog belonged to a Karampas, he shot the dog dead with a pistol saying, "At least we killed one Karampas." I heard the news about my dog in Athens which made me very sad.

LIFE IN ATHENS

Our Temporary Home in Athens

After getting off the boat, we took a train to the center of Athens called Omonia Square, and from there we took a bus to where my Aunt Evgenia and Uncle Nick were staying. It was a stand-alone building that was owned by Uncle Nick's brother who allowed us to live there on a temporary basis. My sister, my cousin Georgia and I stayed there while my father went to stay with the Lyskas family in a southern suburb of Athens. The Lyskas family was the family from whom my parents had bought their first house in Vrontama, and they had maintained a good and close friendship with them throughout the years.

I had never seen a very large city before except Sparta and Tripoli, and going through Athens by train and bus was a real treat for me. I had never seen so many cars and so many people walking in the streets. I saw a policeman directing traffic in some intersections, while in other intersections cars were waiting for a green light in order to go forward. The tall buildings made a big impression on me, and I was wondering how many steps people had to climb in order to go to the floors way above the street level.

When we arrived at our temporary home, I wanted to go to the bathroom and asked my aunt where it was. She directed me to a room with a toilet and a sink. After I used the bathroom, my aunt showed me how to flush the toilet, which was a new experience for me because in the village we did not have any running water for that purpose. For the next several days and weeks, everything I did was a new experience.

The house in which we were staying was close to the center of Athens on a very busy street. I went outside by the front door of the house, walked to the corner and observed the cars, trams and the people who were walking on the street. I wondered who those people were, where they were going and where they were coming from. Little by little, I became more courageous, and with permission from my aunt, I walked down the street for a few blocks in each direction to get acquainted with the neighborhood until I started to feel more comfortable walking in the city streets.

Omonia Square at that time was one of the places in Athens where many people from the villages would congregate and meet other people from their own village to hear the news. Remember that Greece was still fighting a civil war, and many people from the villages had come to Athens to save their lives. The coffeehouse "Neon" was the meeting place where my father and my Uncle John would meet people from Vrontama and hear the news from their village. They would go to this coffeehouse usually in the evening and always on the lookout for anyone who might recognize them and have them arrested on a trumped-up charge. My father wanted me to get adjusted to city life, and many times he would take me with him to the coffeehouse. I really enjoyed going with my dad because this was an opportunity for me to see the city and most importantly to see it at night with all the signs lit up, not to mention that my father would buy me some kind of sweet.

We stayed in that house for two to three months, but when my mother came to Athens, we had to go live somewhere else because that house was not big enough to accommodate all of us. Another reason we had to move was that my Uncle Nick's brother, who was the owner of that house, wanted my dad to start paying some rent which my dad was not able to do.

Our Family Together Again

Potoula's godfather was a teacher at a high school that was located in a southern suburb of Athens called Nea Smyrna. Because I did not have time to study and take the exams to qualify me to enter high school, my sister's godfather intervened for me, and I was enrolled in the seventh grade of the school where he taught.

While I still lived in the first house, I walked to the center of Athens and caught a bus that took me to the square in front of the school. It did not take me long to adjust to that routine, but it did not last. We could not afford to pay rent where my sister and I lived. Fortunately the Lyskas family asked our whole family to move into a two-room apartment that had recently been built for a sister of the family and her husband. She was working as a nurse and staying close to the hospital and her husband's furniture-making business, so at least for that time, they did not need that apartment. They let us stay there without paying rent.

Finally, our family was together again. Along with the immediate family, my Uncle John and my cousin Georgia also stayed with us. Sometimes when my father met someone from the village who did not have a place to stay, he would invite him to stay with us until he found another place to stay. Some of these people who thought that it was safe to return to the village after a few months or a year of staying in Athens were caught and executed within days upon arriving back in the village. The apartment was too small for all of us and not the most comfortable situation, but we were just happy to have a place to stay.

The Lyskas family was very hospitable to all members of our family. During the winter months, they would invite us over to their living quarters next door where they had a heating stove to get warm. We did not have a stove on our side because we were not able to afford one. When we first arrived in Athens, we did not have any dishes or eating utensils. We would borrow them from another family after they finished eating. The Lyskas family gave us an old table, a couple of dishes and utensils so that we could eat whatever my mother was able to cook for all of us. After a month, my cousin Georgia found a job as a nanny and servant in someone's house, and her sister Popi found a job as a seamstress. This helped the sleeping accommodations considerably because now there were only five of us left to share the sleeping floor space instead of seven. We were also happy that Georgia and Popi had found work that provided them with fairly good living quarters. Although they no longer stayed with us, they would come to visit us regularly when they had a day off from their work.

The high school that I was attending was now very close to our new home and within walking distance of about one mile. During recess all the students would go out in front of the school where a few ice cream salesmen and other vendors were waiting for their business. I also went outside, but I never had any money to buy anything. I just sat on the sidewalk and watched the ice cream vendors put the ice cream between two wafers and give it to the students who could afford to buy it. I was very aware that our family's finances did not allow me to have money for ice cream.

Before I left home in the morning, my mother would give me money to buy bread for home on my way back from school. The money was always the same amount because immediately after the war the authorities regulated not only the price of bread, but also how much bread a family could buy. In order for the bakery to know how much bread it could sell to anyone, the city gave each family coupons that had to be shown and punched at the bakery in order to buy the bread in the legal quantity. If the loaf of bread weighed less than the allowed weight, the baker would cut a piece from another loaf and wrap it with the whole loaf of bread to be taken home. If the loaf of bread weighed more, a piece would be cut out in order to meet the allowed weight. Every school day it was my job to stop at the bakery and buy the bread for the day. I always hoped that the baker would give me a piece of bread to compliment the allowable weight because I was always hungry coming home from school and the piece of bread would satisfy my hunger by the time I went home.

One day my father gave me a small amount of extra money and told me to have a little ice cream at recess. The vendor was very surprised when I went to buy ice cream because I always used to stand around and watch the other kids buy ice cream and never bought any myself. He asked me why all of a sudden I was buying ice cream. I told him that I never had any money to buy ice cream or anything else, but that day was the exception because my father had given me some money. I must have touched a nerve with him, and he charged me half the price that everyone else paid. Giving me the ice cream, he told me that if I wanted another one, to see him after school and he would give me one at the same price. After school, I went to see him, and again he gave me another ice cream for half the price. This time, however, I wanted to give the ice cream that I bought to my sister who had never had ice cream before and was at home. Holding it in my hand, I ran toward the house as fast as I could. The ice cream started to melt, but fortunately before I reached home, I saw my sister playing with other girls and I gave her what ice cream was still left between the two wafers. The rest of it I licked from my own hands. Naturally, I had to run back to the bakery and get the bread, but I did not mind that at all. At dinner Potoula told my ice cream story, and my parents were impressed that I thought to bring ice cream to her. They knew then that what they had taught us about loving each other had taken root in us. My father was so moved by my gesture that the following week he gave me enough money to buy ice cream for myself.

After a while, during recess I would go to the ice cream vendor, who was about forty years old and wore old clothes, and visit with him. He told me that during the war he had lost his wife from hunger and had two young daughters who were going to a nearby grade school. He also had come to Athens from one of the Peloponnese provinces for the safety of his daughters. We talked about our families, the occupation during the war, and our villages. He started to trust me after a while, and if he had to leave his station for a few minutes, he would ask me to stay and sell ice cream to anyone who came to buy it. I never took advantage of the situation in his absence. I always gave him a complete accounting of the sales and never asked him to give me anything for helping him. He, however, totally on his own would offer me ice cream during recess telling me that it was a gift from him.

A month after we moved to this house, my father found a job as a night watchman at a nearby fuel depot run by the remnants of the British army that was still in Athens. The entire family was happy that my father found this job. Finally we were able to buy not only meat for the dinner table, but also other things that my mother needed in the kitchen. The fuel depot where my father worked proved to be a very dangerous place to be. Black marketers would climb the fences and force themselves into the depot area to steal barrels of petroleum and anything else they could get their hands on to sell it on the black market. The guards were instructed to shoot at these intruders, but the intruders had more and better weapons. Several watchmen were killed in a matter of days trying to do their job. My father was not too keen on shooting at anyone, and after working there for three months, he quit his job for safety reasons.

My Uncle John was trying to go to America at the invitation of his brother who lived in Middletown, Ohio. Before the war and during the postwar period, the American government allowed only a small number of people from Greece to go to America. Even before the war Uncle John was repeatedly called by the American Embassy for interviews, but he always was told that his number would come up later, and he would return home to Vrontama dejected. Now while in Athens, he continued to believe that he would soon go to America. Unfortunately that time never came. After the end of the civil war, he returned to Vrontama where he married a lady from a nearby village.

Help in Time of Need

Late in 1946 my Uncle Tony came to Athens from Australia where he had lived for twenty years after leaving Kosma. He had left the village to go to Australia in pursuit of better business opportunities as many young men from the village were doing at that time. He is the one who sent several boxes of new shoes after the war to be distributed to the children of the village of Kosma. When he came, our family was living in the Lyskas house, and he was invited to stay with my Aunt Evgenia and Uncle Nick in the central part of Athens. He wanted to go to Kosma to see the village where he was born and grew up, but the family advised him not to go because his life would be in danger.

About the same time that Uncle Tony returned from Australia, the Lyskas's daughter and her husband decided to move to the house in which we were living because the house where they were staying was being torn down. We had to find another place to live which was very difficult especially since we could not pay the two months rent in advance that was needed. Uncle Tony heard about this and helped us by paying the first four months of rent for us. One of my father's friends told him that there was an apartment available for rent in the neighborhood called Sepolia. The whole family went to see this apartment which was on the second floor of a tavern and milk distribution store. The apartment had two rooms, a very small kitchen, and a bathroom that was shared with the two sons of the landlord who lived across the hall. We left the Lyskas family for our new apartment with some very good memories and appreciation for everything that they had done for us in time of desperate need. To this day, I remember the kindness, love and support that they gave to us so generously.

The new apartment had been built recently, but without any plans for heating it. The only heat that we had during the winter was a small stove that was open at the top, with coals providing the heat. Several times we all got up in the morning with severe headaches until my father realized that burning the coal all night in a closed area with no ventilation was taking out the oxygen and leaving carbon monoxide for us to breathe. The decision was then made that the stove would be put out before going to bed, and the headaches went away.

Mrs. Eleni Gravari lived on the next block from our apartment with her son and his friend. Mrs. Eleni came to meet us when we moved into the apartment, and immediately we became good friends with her and her family. We still did not have the necessary things for the kitchen. We only had three plates, three glasses, utensils for three people and only a small pot in which to boil things. Mrs. Eleni noticed our needs and without being asked, she gave us dishes, glasses, utensils and a large pot for boiling food. She also gave us blankets and pillows in order to make our sleeping a little better at night. Mrs. Eleni was also from Vrontama. When she got married, she moved to Athens with her husband. My father knew her family very well, and our families developed a kinship that lasted until my mother and father and Mrs. Eleni and her family died. Her kindness, however, will always remain with me forever and remind me how people should express their love and appreciation to their friends and family in time of need.

The landlord and his wife also had taken an interest in me and my sister. Sometimes they would give us some milk that they had left over in the store below our apartment. Twice in one summer they took us on a picnic by the sea because we told them that we did not know what it was like to go on a picnic by the sea. They packed a basket with bread, feta cheese and olives and went to an area called Marathon, which is the place where the ancient Athenians fought the Persians during the Golden Age of Athens. My sister and I always remember the kindness that that they showed us during the summer of 1947.

In the meantime, my father started to work with his brother George Manos from Middletown, Ohio to import items that were very scarce in Greece at that time, such as used clothing, ladies nylons and antibiotic drugs. Uncle George would buy clothes and other used items from Goodwill and other charities, put them in cardboard barrels and send them to my father and Uncle John. Later he started to buy nylon stockings and send them to my father with visiting friends and relatives to avoid the custom fees which were very high for such items. My father would sell those items at a good profit and return the cost to his brother when someone trustworthy returned to America. At that time, it was illegal to send money out of the country. However, those were desperate times for survival, and at times people had to step outside of the law to feed and protect their families. And so, with help from my uncle in America and my father's aggressive selling, our family's finances improved, and we started to live a little more comfortable life.

Going to School in Athens

When we moved to Sepolia, it was necessary for me to move my school records from the Nea Smyrna High School for Boys that I attended since coming to Athens to the Fourth Gymnasium for Boys extension that was within walking distance from where we lived. This extension had only grades seven and eight, and I eventually completed the remaining seventh grade and the entire eighth grade there. I forgot to mention that all the schools in Athens were separated by gender.

By present standards, the classrooms in the school were rather primitive, but the students and teachers were there for one reason, and that was for the teachers to teach and the students to learn. Corporal punishment for misbehavior was the rule. This made the students aware that bad behavior was not to be tolerated. The parents never interfered with the relationship between teachers and students, unless it had to do with their progress in their academics. I, personally, adjusted well to the new school environment and never had any problems following the school rules.

At that time the second language that everyone wanted to learn was French. It was considered as the language used in business, government, or any other venture that people wanted to pursue in their lives. Therefore, French was taught in Greek high schools everywhere. I was not doing very well in my French class, and my grades in that class showed it. The teacher was very good and was trying to help me do better. My father decided that if I was going to succeed in life, I had to learn French. He enrolled me and my sister in a French tutoring class in which I did a little better. Although I was not totally happy attending it, I did well enough to get a decent grade in high school which pleased my parents. My sister, on the other hand, did extremely well, and to this day she is fluent in French. She eventually worked for Air France in the personnel department and later was promoted to the position of Personnel Manager.

Upon completion of the eighth grade, I had to start attending classes at the main Fourth Gymnasium for Boys. The school was located off one of the streets out of Omonia Square. Most of the time, I took the bus to Omonia and then walked down to the street where the school was located. Sometimes, in order to save the bus fare, I took the back roads to school. My classes had become more difficult than the previous year, but I learned how to cope and did well in all of my classes.

A student had to take the courses that were required for each grade. These classes included Modern Greek, Ancient Greek, French, Mathematics, Physics, Religion, Geography, etc. I always had homework to do after going home, and my father made sure that I completed it and correctly. There were no extracurricular activities sponsored by the school, but I played ball and other games in the neighborhood after I completed my homework. That was the school where I completed the ninth and tenth grade.

New Experiences

At the beginning of 1948, our landlord needed the apartment where we were staying for one of his sons who lived across the hall in the small apartment with his brother and asked us to find another place to live. Mrs. Eleni, whom my father would refer to as our angel from God, told us of another apartment that was available only a block and a half away. We all went to see it. It had one large room, a small kitchen, and a bathroom outside of the kitchen next to the storage of wood needed for the landlord's potbelly stove. The rent was half of what we had been paying, and my parents decided to take it. They told me and my sister that this would allow us to save more money and eventually get our own place. We moved the few things that we had and made the one room apartment our new home. Because the apartment was so small, my Uncle John moved to another area in Athens where he rented a room for himself. This left our immediate family to live in this apartment by ourselves for the first time since we left the village.

By now we had accumulated the necessities needed such as beds, a dinner table and chairs. My mom and dad had their own bed, my sister had a single bed, and I had an old army cot to sleep on. My parents' bed was placed on the southwest corner of the room, my sister's bed along the south wall, and my cot along the east and south walls. The dinner table was placed in the middle of the room with five chairs around. It was not the ideal situation, but we learned to cope with it and were happy living there. The only time we had a problem was when my father found someone from our village at the coffeehouse in Omonia who did not have a place to stay and brought him home to stay with us until he found a place. It was not unusual for such a visitor to stay with us for several days.

Two or three such people were not able to adjust to city life and returned to the village only to be executed by the militia thugs from Mani.

The most uncomfortable situation in our apartment was that of the bathroom. First, there was no toilet. Instead, in the place where the commode is usually located, there was a three by three foot tile with a hole in the middle for the waste to drop into. To make things worse, there was not a door to provide any privacy. This facility was also used by the landlord's family. We all learned when approaching the bathroom to make noise with our shoes, so if anyone was using it at the time, they would cough telling the person outside that the toilet was in use. This also did not bother us after a while, and we learned how to cope with it.

Our landlord's son Elias and I quickly became good friends and spent most of our free time together playing soccer with other neighborhood kids at a nearby open field. I had never played soccer before, and Elias taught me how to play. In the summertime when it was too hot to play soccer, we played checkers, marbles and other games in the small courtyard of the house shaded by trees.

In the summer of 1948, my cousins Katherine and Mary Kara, who at that time lived in Middletown, Ohio with my Uncle George Manos, sent me a two-wheeled scooter. Looking at this gift with the eyes of a fourteen-year-old, I could not believe that someone had sent me such a wonderful gift that was actually mine. I immediately took it out on the street, and after falling off of it a few times, I shared it with my friend Elias, his brother and some other children in the neighborhood. The next day my father told me to sit down and write a letter to my cousins in America to thank them for this wonderful gift. I considered that scooter my most prized possession and used it until the day that I left Greece for America.

Once in a while my mother would send me to the main market in the center of Athens to buy fruit, tomatoes, fish and other things for the house. That was usually my father's job, but my mother would send me when my father was not available. I actually looked forward to performing that function because it made me feel like I was responsible enough to be trusted in making a contribution to the family's well-being. However, things did not work out well for me all the time.

Some vendors in the market were not very honest, especially when the customer was a young kid. I would handpick the tomatoes or grapes that I wanted, and the vendor would take the bag to weigh it. If a customer was not watching what the vendor was doing, he would switch what the customer had picked out with another bag that contained inferior merchandise. I was fooled by a vendor twice before I learned my lesson. Each time I went home my mother would carefully inspect the quality of goods that I was told to buy. Twice she was upset with me and told me that I had wasted the money she had given me. She was so upset with me that she took the bag that I had brought home and hit me over the head with it leaving squash, tomatoes and sour grapes on my head. After those two times, I learned my lesson well and never allowed myself to be fooled again. Shopping for the fish that my mother wanted was much easier for me. The fish in the market were last night's catch, and I always went to buy the fish early in the morning. The family was always happy with the fish I selected. I do not recall the types of the fish, but they were of the type that we could afford.

During the Christmas and New Year's holidays, Elias and I decided to go around the homes and sing Greek carols in order to make some money. We both got a metal triangle and started going to the houses around the neighborhood asking the people if they wanted us to sing the carols called "kalanda" for Christmas and the following week, for New Year. The people realized that if they said "yes," they would have to give us a little money. Only a few of them would say "yes" and give us something. We were not doing that well in our neighborhood and had to make a strategic decision. The people in our neighborhood were not rich, and that was the reason for not being generous. We had to go to neighborhoods where people had more money and could afford to tip us better. And so we went to some of the more affluent areas, rang the door bells, and asked the lady of the each house if we could say the kalanda, as was the custom at the time. Most of the time not only did people let us sing, but some of the people also gave us pastries and a glass of water to drink. Within five hours, we had accumulated lots of money by our standards and stopped because of darkness. We came back home, sat around our table, counted our money, and then divided it between us. I went to bed that night thinking about what to do with the money that I had and how to tell my father after I made my decision. Would he tell me to give him the money for use by the entire family? Or would he allow me to use it for something that I wanted?

I had never had a bicycle to learn how to ride one. I made the decision that if my father allowed me to do something with the money that I wanted to do, I would go to a shop that rented bicycles and rent one for two hours. The next day I told my father about my decision, and he complimented me for my choice. I remember to this day that he told me that I should gain experience in doing many things in order to learn how to cope in modern life. He even told me that if I were older, he would even support me in learning to drive a car. I thanked my father and headed to the bike shop to rent a bike which I did not know how to ride.

I went to the bike rental shop and paid to rent the bike for two hours. The owner did not ask me if I knew how to ride the bike. I walked the bike to my neighborhood, and with some help from other kids who knew how to ride a bike, I was able to ride it for short distances at the beginning and longer rides a little later. I fell a few times and scraped my legs, but I was determined to become a good rider, so that did not bother me. As my confidence increased, I started going much faster than I should have, and when I took a right turn onto a narrow street with a five-foot drop on its side, I fell into it which caused a flat tire on the bike. My time was almost up for the bike rental, and I returned the bike to the shop. Naturally they charged me for repairing the flat tire, and I went home to face my mother with the scrapes on my knees and legs. My mother was not there at the time, and that gave me a chance to wash and wear clean clothes in order to avoid a lecture.

The following week Elias and I decided to go out this time to sing the customary kalanda for the New Year. Once again we went to a more affluent neighborhood than ours where the people had been very generous to us the previous week. We came home with about the same money that we had collected for singing the Christmas carols. I saved my share and used it to go to the outdoor theater "Hollywood" that was nearby. This made me feel a little independent because I did not have to ask my father for money. I always told my father when I went to the theater, and I had to have his approval on the type of movie that I was going to see. That was when I saw two or three "Tarzan" movies with my friends. We all thought that the "Tarzan" movies were the greatest movies that we had ever seen.

My Leg Problem Returns

In 1947, I started to have problems with the leg that had been infected with osteomyelitis during the war. I was experiencing pain, some drainage and some swelling which would go away in a few days, only to return again in a few weeks. The doctors would give me different injections that helped the inflammation, but did nothing to cure the chronic infection. There was not an effective antibiotic medication for this problem in Greece at that time. Penicillin, which would treat this condition, was available in America but not in Greece. Therefore, the inflammation kept coming back, and each time with more intensity. The doctors recommended that my father take me to America for better treatment.

In order to go to America for any reason, someone in America had to sponsor me and my dad and vouch that we would not become a burden to the government while in America. My Uncle George Lambros, my mother's brother who lived in Valparaiso, Indiana, made a formal invitation through the State Department for me and my dad to come to America so that I could receive the much needed medical treatment.

At that time the American Embassy was very thorough in investigating everyone who wanted to come to America for any reason. The town council of Vrontama was asked to provide the embassy with an affidavit about my father's character. The self-appointed council in Vrontama notified the American Embassy that my father was a Communist and a criminal and that he was wanted for crimes that were committed during the war. These charges, of course, were not true. At the embassy's invitation, my father went to dispute the report from our village.

Camping at Salamis Island

While waiting to hear what the embassy would decide about my father, I went to summer camp. In the postwar years the Greek government sponsored children of my age to go camping for one month on the island of Salamis at no expense to the parents. This was only available for children living in the inner city. Going to an inner city school, I qualified to go camping for one month. The school that I attended notified the students who wanted to go so that they would sign up for camp. I signed up for camp in 1948, 1949 and 1950, and all three years I was lucky enough to attend the camp.

I really enjoyed going to this camp which was attended by about 100 to 150 children with several counselors at each camp site. The counselors did a very good job of organizing activities for the entire day which included swimming in the ocean, hiking, and campfire activities which always included singing Greek songs popular at the time, etc. The activities that I enjoyed the most were swimming in the morning and hiking in the afternoon to the top of the mountain to see the place where the famous Battle of Salamis had taken place between the Athenians and the Persians. We went swimming at different parts of the island. We usually went swimming in the morning hours and came back to camp looking forward to having our noon meal which was not always to everyone's liking. We had to eat what we were given, but I don't remember anyone who did not eat because of not liking the food. Meals were served to everyone at the same time, and every day the kids from one of the tents had to peel the potatoes and clean the metal trays on which everyone ate. The camp was made up of eight tents with every tent housing sixteen boys. The counselors organized the kitchen duty on a rotating basis so that boys from each tent were responsible for that duty. Every afternoon after the two-hour siesta, which was mandatory, we were all gathered in the middle of the camp area and given our hiking assignment. I enjoyed all the activities to the fullest and made many friends, some of whom came to the camp annually like I did.

In July 1950 my father came to camp unexpectedly to see me. When I saw him, I thought that he was going to tell me some kind of bad news concerning our family. With permission from the camp counselor, he took me to a nearby restaurant and told me the news that he was rejected by the American Embassy to go to America with me, but the embassy would let me go by myself if I wanted to go. He explained to me that if I wanted to get well, that was the best option for me. I had two choices: stay in Greece and suffer with pain in my right leg or go to America, hoping to get better. I asked my dad if my mother agreed for me to go to America, and his answer was positive. I thought for awhile, and then I told my father that if he and Mom thought that going to America for treatment was the best solution, I would agree to go. My father left the camp, but my conversation with him never left my mind. I became very sad that I was going to leave my country, my parents, my school and my friends and go to a country whose language, people, and customs I did not know. I had to leave everything that was familiar to me, but I made up my mind to go to America, as unfamiliar as it was to me, for one reason: to get well and come back to my family healthy.

Trip Preparations

When camp was over, I returned to Athens where my neighborhood friends had learned about my pending trip to America. They kept telling me that our separation would be only for a year and I would be coming back home before I knew it. My father had started the process for my visa through the American Embassy, and my mother was gathering the clothes that I was to take with me for my trip. At that time, ready-made suits could not be found in stores. If someone wanted a suit, it would have to be made by a tailor. I had never had a suit to wear, so my father took me to a tailor to have a suit made for me. Fortunately, a few days before, we had received some fabric from my uncle in Middletown, Ohio which we used for this suit. I now had a suit to wear on my trip.

In the meantime the husband of my Aunt Marigo from Valparaiso had died in June 1950, and two months later my Uncle George Lambros, who had invited me to America for medical treatment, also died unexpectedly. That was something that we did not want the American Embassy to know. If the embassy knew of his death, they could withdraw my visa because it would leave me without a sponsor.

At that same time, my father had the opportunity of buying a lot close to the neighborhood where we had lived before moving to our current one-room apartment. The negotiated price was 100 English gold pounds which at that time was a lot of money. However, with sacrifices that the family had made in the last three years and with the commerce in which my father was involved with my Uncle George Manos in America, he was able to get the money and buy that lot. I remember going with my father to close the deal and then to find a surveyor who certified that the lot was legitimate and within the city plans. But buying the lot took the money that was to pay for my trip to America. My father asked my Uncle George to send him the money for my trip with the understanding that the money would be returned to him from the profits he expected to have from the sale of goods my uncle was sending him. My uncle agreed and the travel agency booked me to fly out of Athens on September 25, 1950 with British Airways.

My Farewell Trip to Vrontama

The civil war continued to take its toll on the people of Vrontama until the middle of 1949. My father and my Uncle John were still targets for assassination by the militia gangs that continued to roam the villages in our area. Therefore, if my father and Uncle John were to go Vrontama to see their father, the risk of being killed was very high.

On March 29, 1949, we were notified by my father's sister that my grandfather had died. My father and Uncle John weighed the option of going home for the funeral, but their sister and their cousins told them that if they did go, they would be killed. For several years after my grandfather's death, my father carried the burden in his heart of not being able to help his father when he needed him. As for me, I was very sad and my mind kept going to the last time I had seen my grandfather when we had said our goodbyes in the middle of the night. I was sad that after being an altar boy for most of my life and having accompanied the funeral processions of so many other people to the cemetery, I was not able to be there for my grandfather.

By the spring of 1950 things had quieted down in Vrontama, and in anticipation of my going to America, I went to Vrontama to pay my respects at my grandfather's grave. I went to the cemetery with a brush and some black paint and painted my grandfather's name on the cross on top of his grave. That was the cemetery where I had gone so many times before as an altar boy with Fr. Vassilis to bury the dead. I became quite emotional when I started to think about the many people who had been killed and buried there during the dark days of the civil war that plagued my hometown. I still remembered most of those good people from the days when our village was so united in fighting the enemy during the war.

My pending trip to America was kept secret from everyone in the village except our very close relatives. If the people who still hated my father knew about it, they could still notify the American Embassy not to give me a visa because I was the son of someone whom they had labeled a Communist.

The Long Goodbye

During the week before my anticipated departure, we were visited by many family friends, relatives and several people from our village living in Athens who came to say goodbye to me and to tell me to give their regards to their own relatives in America. Although my parents and my sister were all happy about me going to America for medical treatment, there was also a sadness present in all of us and especially in my mother whom I had seen crying when no one was looking. When I saw her, I always went to her, crying myself, and tried to console her by telling her that I would soon be back from America when my treatment was over.

My mother kept three or four chickens outside of our apartment in order to have fresh eggs. She would feed them, clean the chicken coup every week and bring the fresh eggs in as soon as they were laid by the chickens. We had the chickens for the sole purpose of having fresh eggs and never cooked them. The last day before I was to leave was the exception. My mother picked one of the chickens and cooked it for my last dinner at home. Besides the chicken, she prepared some fish, potatoes and salad and invited our closest relatives and some very close friends for dinner. Everyone was encouraging me that I would enjoy being in America and would get well with all the medical means that were available there. After dinner, as people were leaving and saying their goodbyes, my mother became emotional and started to cry and tell everyone that America would seduce me with all its riches to keep me there.

Before going to bed, my mother opened an old suitcase and put in it my underwear which took only a limited amount of space. This left most of the suitcase empty, and in order to fill it, she picked two blankets that she had made by hand and put them in the suitcase along with four bottles of Metaxas Cognac as gifts for my uncle and my aunt in Valparaiso, giving me specific instructions on their distribution.

I was not able to sleep at all. I tossed and turned all night, and the movie in my mind never stopped. It kept playing the events that I had experienced in my life, the love of my family, my friends, my neighbors, my teachers, schoolmates, etc. The movie in my head brought everything to me as if everything was happening right at that moment. I cried quietly and started to question my decision of going to America. Then I thought of my leg problem which had to be taken care of in order to live a normal life. I was thinking of the next day's goodbyes and how sad all of us would be. So I just continued to toss and turn until the light of day came through the shutters of the window next to my bed.

Everyone got up early that morning. Even the landlord's family, with whom we had become good friends, got up and asked if their son Elias, my friend, could come to the airport with my family to see me off. Soon my Uncle John and my cousin Georgia came to the house so that they could also go to the airport. I wore my new suit for the first time, and I looked at myself thinking, "Is this how the Americans dress?"

My father had bought an agenda book for 1950. It was a small, pocket-sized book with a map of Greece and Athens and every page containing three days of each month with enough space to write short notes under each day. He asked me to sit with him at the dinner table because he wanted to talk to me about things that I should know and follow in life while I was away from home. That was the first time that my father and I had a one-on-one talk. I really did not know what to expect. He opened the agenda book and asked me to read a page which was written in his own handwriting. What I read was profound advice that only a parent could pass on to his son. He had written the following:

> Always be honorable
> Be honest
> Work hard
> Have courage facing life
> Honor and respect your elders
> Be compassionate
> Be a good conversationalist
> Be observant and exercise good judgment
> Love to learn and educate yourself
> Never forget your mother country and your family
> Always correspond with your family and
>   be descriptive in what you write
> Always be humble and not an egoist
> Always be thankful to people who help you and
>   never be ungrateful
> Always love, respect and fear God

My father told me to take the agenda book and look at the above whenever I had doubts about myself or life in general. I still have that agenda book and occasionally I still read my father's advice. We did not have material things that I could take with me, but in my opinion, that was the best thing that I was ever given by my parents, and it has lasted a lifetime.

My father had a taxi come to the house to take me, my parents, my sister and Uncle John to the travel agency office that was located on Constitution Square. Everyone else took the bus, and we all met outside the British Airways office next door. After my passport was checked, I was told to go onto a bus that would take me to the airport. Everyone else had to take public transportation to the airport. We all met again and my father took some pictures with an old camera he had.

The time had come to face the hardest thing that I had ever experienced in my life. I was embraced and kissed by everyone. All of us were crying, especially my mother who embraced me and would not let me go to board the plane. It was heartbreaking for my mother to let me go. After surviving the war and all the struggles that followed, she was losing her son to a foreign country. Although we all expected me to return when my leg was healed, perhaps she knew, as only a mother knows, that her little boy would never come back to live with the family again.

A stewardess came over, took me by the hand, led me to the bottom of the steps to the plane and asked me to go up. I turned around to see my parents for the last time, and with tears in my eyes, I was able to see the white hankies that they were waving at me. The door of the plane closed and suddenly I felt lonely and isolated. I felt that the closing of the door was a sign that I was about to enter a new phase in my life. I was leaving behind me everything that I had treasured in my young life to go to a place unknown to me.

I looked in my pocket and found the agenda book that my father had given me a few hours earlier. I started to read what he had written, and my eyes went to the paragraph saying that I should face life with courage. I read it a few times, and I began to understand that this was the right time for me to start facing life with courage. I was only sixteen years old, but I realized that from now on I had to be in charge of myself, and to do that, I had to face the future as an adult. I shook the despair out of my head and made up my mind to start facing life as it comes.

My parents 1933

My parents, Grandfather Karampas and me 1935

Grandfather Karampas and me
1936

Grandfather Lambros and me
1936

My sister Potoula and me
1942

The Italian, Domenick

Uncle John, Uncle Nick, me, Mom, Potoula, Aunt Alexandra,
Aunt Evgenia and Uncle Tony in Athens

8th Grade, 2nd row, 3rd from right

Last day in Athens 1950

My father, his brother John,
his sisters Katie and Lygeri

Passport photo 1950

A New Life in America

The Trip to America

The plane was a two-engine propeller plane. Inside there were two rows of seats: two seats on one side of the aisle and one seat on the other. The stewardess took me to the single seat row. I kept looking out of the window with sadness as the plane was taking off. The stewardess came by several times to talk to me, but since I didn't speak English, I did not understand what she was telling me. I assumed that she was trying to encourage me. After sitting in the plane for one hour, I had to go to the bathroom. Fortunately, I heard a man and a woman speaking Greek. I asked them if there was a bathroom and they showed me where it was. When I returned, I tried to make conversation with them, but I got the impression that they did not want to talk to me. I went to my seat and sat there until our first stop at Nice, France.

We were asked to get off the plane for half an hour. The stewardess came and motioned to me that I was supposed to follow everyone else to the terminal. I saw the passengers going to a snack bar, but I had two problems: one, I did not know how to order anything, and two, even if I had known how to order something, I did not have any money. So I stayed by the door and followed the other passengers to the plane at boarding time.

Our next stop was London, England. I really had no idea what my itinerary was. I just followed everybody else off the plane and went to the terminal, wondering where my suitcase was. Once again, I found the Greek-speaking people from our plane, and they pointed to the place where I could find my suitcase, which I found waiting for me. A young woman wearing an airline uniform took me to a bus and stayed with me until it stopped in front of what looked like a very old hotel with bullet holes on the outside. I enjoyed the trip from the airport to the city because it gave me the opportunity to see a city larger than Athens and see the people walking in the streets with different types of clothing than people in Athens wore. Fall had come to London and the people had started to wear heavy clothes. I saw several buildings that were severely damaged and others that were torn down. The bombing during the war was evident and also the reconstruction of the city. For the first time I saw two-level buses which were so tall that I wondered how they were able to go under the bridges.

Upon arrival at the hotel, I was escorted to the lobby by the young lady, and someone from the hotel took me to a large room where several people were sitting around tables. That was the hotel's restaurant. I looked at the clock on the wall, and the time was 9:00 p.m. which reminded me that it was dinner time. Someone came to ask me what I wanted, and seeing the food that some of the other people had in front of them, I pointed to a dish across the table which looked like a cheese sandwich. By this time, I was so hungry that I did not care what they brought me to eat. They brought me a ham and cheese sandwich which was enough to satisfy my appetite. Through hand signals, I was told that it was time to go to sleep. The next day I was to leave for America.

I was led to a large room, which looked like an army barracks, with several two-level bunks set up in two rows. I was shown a large bathroom facility that had a shower but not a single towel in it. The man that led me to that room told me to sleep in any one of the beds because I was the only one there. I slept on one of the lower bunks. I was very tired with everything new that I had experienced that day. I was a little scared at the beginning because I was the only one sleeping in such a large room by myself in a strange place, but I tried to put everything aside and fell asleep with the lights on. In the morning, I was awakened by the squeaky sound of a door opening and saw a man coming in to wake me up. He motioned to me that I should go downstairs after I got dressed. I did not have a towel with me, but I went to the sink in the bathroom, washed my face with soap and water, and dried it with some paper towels available in a basket. I picked up my suitcase and went downstairs where I was led to a small lunch room where I was served corn flakes with milk and orange juice. After breakfast, everybody was led to a bus that took us to the airport. Following the other people, I boarded a much larger plane with six seats across divided by an aisle. It was a BOAC which stood for British Overseas Airways Corporation.

Our first stop was at Shannon, Ireland to refuel. We were told that we could get out of the plane and go to the terminal if we wanted. Being somewhat curious and wanting to see as many different places as possible, I went to the terminal to walk around and see interesting things in another strange place without it costing me anything. We boarded the plane again, knowing that our next stop was New York. The service on the plane was very good, and the food we were served was even better. That made this leg of the trip so pleasant that my apprehension about going to America had faded.

Arriving in New York

We arrived at New York International Airport at 9:30 in the morning. I followed everyone else as they were getting out of the plane. There was a woman dressed in some kind of an official uniform who was asking everyone in the line questions. Some people were directed to the right and others to the left. She did not ask me any questions, and I followed the people going to the right which, I found out later, was the line for American citizens.

I walked to a glass-enclosed booth where a man asked questions that I did not understand, and I kept looking at him with a puzzled look. He looked at my Greek passport and asked the woman in uniform to take me to the end of the line on the left. There, I showed my passport, and the man in the booth asked me questions that again I did not understand. I felt like a blind person being led from one location to another. That was the specific moment that I pledged to myself that I was going to learn English as quickly as possible. The immigration person asked to have someone who spoke the Greek language come to his booth. I felt somewhat more at ease when a man came and talked to me in Greek. He just asked me why I was coming to America and if someone was here to receive me. I told him the reason for coming and that my cousin Peter Kara who lived in New York was supposed to be waiting for me.

The man in the booth stamped my passport and asked the Greek-speaking man to escort me until I was in the terminal where my cousin was to meet me. First, he took me to get my suitcase and then to the terminal to meet a cousin that I had never met and would only recognize from pictures. The man asked me to look around for a familiar person. After seeing no one that looked familiar to me, he took me at the BOAC desk and left me there. I stayed by the desk for about half an hour just looking around until a stewardess took me by the hand and told me to sit down in a seat in the waiting room. By now the time was 12:00 noon. There I was in a strange place waiting with my suitcase for someone I had never met to come find me.

I sat in the same seat for an hour, and then I decided to move to another seat that would give me a different view of the terminal. I wanted to absorb as much of the American scene as I could. What made the biggest impression on me, after watching hundreds of people walking around the terminal in a hurry, was the women. They looked tall and wore high heels that made them look even taller and they dressed in nice clothes. Most of the men wore hats, carried briefcases and were mostly in a hurry. For the first time I saw black people, men and women going about their business just like the white people with one exception: everyone who came to sweep the floor or pick up the trash was black. One of the cleaning people came by and talked to me several times. I did not understand what he was telling me, but I had the impression that he was trying to help me. One time he came by and asked me, by gesturing, if I wanted to go to the bathroom. I had not gone since before leaving the plane, and I nodded my head yes. He showed me where the men's room was and stayed by my suitcase until I returned. I was really impressed by his gesture of kindness. Not having anything to give him, I just shook his hand and nodded telling him thank you.

I stayed in the terminal for several hours watching and observing everything and everyone around me. I was getting very hungry, but I had no money to buy any food, so I just waited for someone to tell me what was happening. At 3:30 P.M. someone from the BOAC desk came and asked me to follow him to the desk. He handed me a telephone and I heard someone who identified himself as Peter Kara. He told me that he was not able to make it to the airport to pick me up but that my Uncle George Manos was on a plane from Dayton for that purpose. I was told to go back to my seat and wait. In the meantime my hunger was becoming more intense. I made up my mind to ignore it by practicing the mind over body principle. After all, that type of discipline helped us during the war.

At about 7:00 P.M. a young stewardess came, and taking me by the hand, she took me and my suitcase to a bus. She sat with me, and with hand gestures told me that she was taking me to New York City. Of course, that made me much happier, and I started to enjoy the scenery as the bus headed toward the city. I did not know what to expect in New York, but whatever it was, it had to be better than waiting in the airline terminal.

The bus pulled into a large building called Port Authority, and the stewardess took me by the hand and led me out of the bus. Just as my foot touched the ground, I finally saw a person who was familiar to me from pictures. I immediately recognized my father's older brother who went by the name George Manos, although his real name was Panayiotes Karampas. He also recognized me from pictures that my father had sent to him. After we embraced each other, my uncle tipped the stewardess for bringing me to the city, and the first thing that he asked me was if I was hungry.

He asked a taxi to take us to Peter Kara's apartment that happened to be almost across from the Radio City Theater. We took the elevator to Peter's apartment where I met Peter for the first time. He was a very congenial man and had a good sense of humor. He apologized for not being at the airport. He was a musician and had come home very late the night before and did not wake up until later that afternoon. Both Peter and my uncle were asking me all kinds of questions about relatives in Greece. After a while, they saw that I did not feel that well, and they took me to a restaurant for dinner at about 10:00 P.M. My uncle ordered for me, and a little later the waiter brought a steak, some vegetables and French fries for me to eat. He also brought me a large glass of Coca-Cola, which I had never had or even seen before. We had carbonated drinks in Greece, but they were nothing like Coke. I cannot remember what the others had because I was too busy eating. All I can remember is that I ate that steak so fast that I was finished while the others were just starting to eat their dinner.

After dinner they took me for a walk in the city to show me New York by night. In some strange way, the city looked just as I expected. I was more impressed with the restaurants and all the food than with the neon lights and grandeur of Fifth Avenue. For most of my life, having enough food to eat had been a major concern. In America there was abundant food everywhere, and I was a typical teenage boy who had never had enough to eat. I was surprised, however, at the number of people in the streets at almost midnight.

My uncle suggested that they take me to Peter's apartment to sleep. Just before we got to the apartment, we passed by a place that had a machine that would take pictures of people after they put money in it. My uncle told me that we should take a picture to always remember my first day in America. We got into the booth, put a quarter in the machine, and in seconds a picture came out. As soon as we arrived at the apartment, I was shown the bed where I could sleep. As soon as I laid on it, I must have passed out. I did not wake up until the next morning.

Sightseeing in New York

The next morning I found my uncle in the living room waiting for me to wake up. Peter was still sleeping, and I was told to move around the apartment quietly. Peter was the leader of a Greek-American band; he worked in the evenings and most of the time his engagement was not over until well past midnight. This had become a sore point with my Uncle George because Peter would stay out much later than necessary which resulted in sleeping well into the afternoon. Complaining about this, Uncle George was always telling Peter that he made the night into day and the day into night. That schedule did not allow Peter to be more aggressive in securing engagements or other potential business opportunities. This, as I learned later, was always a point of contention between the two of them.

After I cleaned up, my uncle took me to a restaurant to have something to eat. The restaurant was kind of unusual even by my own inexperienced standards. The first thing that I noticed was that there was no one around to serve us. Then I noticed that the customers would pick up a tray and guide it across a narrow metal slide that was located in front of a metal structure with small windows in it. People would insert a coin under a window, a small door would open and the customers would take out the food or drink that they had chosen. Sliding their trays, the customers went down the line and repeated the process until they had everything they wanted.

Uncle George and I followed this process ourselves and started to look for a table where we could sit down. All the tables were taken and almost full with customers with the exception of one table for four that was occupied by a young, black woman. My uncle appeared to be somewhat reluctant to sit with that black woman, but not having any other choice, we sat at her table after he asked her if we could share the table with her. My uncle told me in Greek that it was not considered proper for white people to sit at the same table with someone who was black. I asked him "why" and he just told me that it was the custom. The woman started to talk to us and was asking my uncle about me. I could not understand what she was telling my uncle, but she gave me the impression that she spoke very well, with a smile and a very pleasant expression on her face. She finished eating before us, and before she left, she took my hand and told me something that was translated to me as wishing me good luck in America. Between this black woman and the black man who tried to help me at the airport, my opinion about the blacks had become very positive.

Leaving the restaurant, we walked to the Empire State Building and took the elevator to the top of the building. The elevator ride was fascinating to me because it was going up so fast that my ears got plugged and my stomach started to get upset. When we reach the top, I felt as though I were standing on top of the world. Looking down to the street, I could see the yellow cabs that looked like small toys while the people walking on the streets could barely be seen.

Leaving the Empire State Building, we went to see some friends of my uncle who had come from our village Vrontama many years ago. They were operating a flower shop in the center of New York. They had never returned to their homeland and wanted me to tell them whatever news I could from Vrontama. One of the men was the brother of a man whose house was near my grandfather's and who was one of the people in Vrontama who had caused the death of many innocent people during the civil war.

My uncle told me that in the early 1900s, when he came to America, he worked with these men in the flower shop until he left New York. This led me to asking him questions as to why he left New York and why he changed his name from Panayiotis Karampas to George Manos. He was taken by surprise by my questions, and we stopped at a nearby coffee shop where he answered my questions.

He was drafted into service at the early stages of World War I and sent to a garrison in New Jersey for training. There were not enough rifles for training, and the recruits had to be trained with broom sticks. They had not even trained with real guns when the orders came for them to be shipped to Europe to fight in the war. Thinking that his group was so inexperienced, with no training at all in using guns, that they would certainly be killed right away, he decided to go AWOL. Obviously he could not return to New York, so he decided to go to Ohio to find the Revelos brothers in Middletown. He went there because the Revelos and Karampas families in Vrontama were not only related, but also very good friends. In Middletown, he changed his name to George Manos and felt safe from being arrested for desertion. He worked for the Revelos brothers until he set up his own business. After a few years, he started to buy pinball machines and put them in restaurants and bars in Middletown and other cities in the area. They proved to be very profitable and eventually he was able to buy his own home in Middletown.

During the war he worked very hard for the War Bond and the War Relief Drives which helped his stature in the city with business and city officials. After the war he put his efforts toward helping our family in Greece with shipments of goods that my father could sell to support our family. This started in 1947 and continued until after I came to America. George Manos was really the savior of our family after the war when we were left with nothing. We all appreciated everything that he did for us.

The next day, we took a taxi to the New York financial district where I was shown the New York Stock Exchange building. We did not go inside. At that time I really did not have an appreciation of what takes place in that building. It was later when I was a college student that I learned what work went on in that building. Across the street there was a shop, and the owner who happened to be outside recognized my uncle and started waving his hands at us. He and my uncle had not seen each other for years, and when they met, they embraced each other and started to talk about the old days in Vrontama. I was introduced to him as a newcomer, and the owner of the store treated us to lunch at the restaurant next door. Going back to his store, Uncle George bought several dozen razors and razor blades which were destined for Greece after we went to Middletown.

Our next stop was to visit the NBC television studio that was close to Peter Kara's apartment. I had never seen a television before, and I was really happy to see the studios of NBC along with several other visitors. It was a guided tour of the entire facility, and I enjoyed seeing everything even though I did not understand anything that the tour guide said. I was even put in front of a television camera and was asked questions that I did not understand. That and the Empire State Building were the highlights of my stay in New York. When we went back to the apartment, I wrote a card to my family telling them about my visit to New York and especially about my television experience. My Uncle George was very generous to me during our stay in New York, and I started to feel comfortable with him. I appreciated his efforts of taking me around the city and trying to help me adjust to being in America.

Going to Middletown

The next day we took a taxi to the airport from where we flew to Dayton, Ohio. It was the end of September 1950, and while we left New York with sunshine and beautiful weather, we found that the weather in Dayton was completely the opposite. It was overcast, raining and cold. Uncle George told me that he had left his car at the airport. That was something special for me because that would be the first time that I was going to ride in a car actually owned by a family member. After getting in the car, a 1950 Ford, we drove through Dayton and stopped at a restaurant just south of the city to have breakfast. That is where I was introduced to American pancakes.

When we arrived at my uncle's house, Peter's sisters, my cousins Katherine and Mary, came to the door to greet us. I recognized them from pictures, and they welcomed me in the house with such grace and smiles that I immediately felt as if I had known them forever. The first thing that I said to them was "thank you" in Greek for sending me the scooter after the war. I was led to the bedroom where I was supposed to sleep and asked if I wanted to lie down and relax for a while. The bedroom had two single beds in it, and I asked if I was sharing the room with someone else. I was told that the room was only for me which impressed me because this was the first time that I not only had a real bed to myself, but also a whole bedroom as well. I was not really tired, so Katherine took me around and gave me a tour of the house. My uncle's bedroom had a bathroom and a shower just for him, and I was shown the bathroom that my cousins and I were to share. We all spent the rest of the day visiting and talking about our families here and in Greece. My cousins seemed very concerned about my health because I was skinny, and they asked me to tell them about my favorite foods. I told them that any type of food was my favorite. Later in the afternoon, I became noticeably tired and asked to go to bed.

I must have had nightmares during the night. My swinging arms got caught in the cord leading to the lamp next to my bed and pulled the lamp off its table. The sound of the lamp falling and breaking woke me up. I did not know what to do. I was embarrassed coming to somebody's home for the first time and breaking something so beautiful. When I woke up in the morning, I told everyone what had happened, and they told me that they already knew and not to worry about it. I was told that it was Sunday and was asked if I wanted to go to church with them. I did want to go, so we got in the car and drove to a very small church on Middletown's First Avenue.

Meeting People in Middletown

The church was in a very small building, and above the entrance there was a sign with the church's name: Sts. Constantine and Helen Greek Orthodox Church. The inside of the church seemed even smaller when I saw it. The sanctuary of the church was full with most of the people standing. People inside the church were turning around looking at me when I walked in with my cousins and my uncle. I realized that to them I was a complete stranger. I felt intimidated, but after a while I started to concentrate more on the Liturgy which was in Greek and it did not bother me. The only thing that was different from the Liturgy in Greece was that the choir did most of the singing, while the chanter only read the Epistle. In Greece, all the singing was done by the chanter.

When the service was over and we walked outside, many of the parishioners were introduced to me by my uncle, Katherine and Mary. I found all of them very friendly, and they were encouraging me that it would not take me long to learn the English language. Besides the people that I already knew, I saw a lady that I had met in Greece only a few months before. She was Thea Frosine Revelos who had visited Greece in the spring and had come to our house to meet my parents at the request of my uncle. She came to greet me and introduced me to her son Charlie. After a while I met her other sons Chris and Mike, her daughter Lula and another young man named Jim Demetrion. I could not get over the fact that all the people that I met that day were so friendly and wanted to talk to me and encourage me as a newcomer. Other people that I met that morning were Jim Revelos with his twin daughters Mary Lou and Martha, John Revelos and Thea Efthemia and their daughter Dolores, the Laras family, the Pantel family, the Valen family, and the Hagias family. Mrs. Hagias had come from Vrontama and was somehow related to my father.

I also met Thea Sophia and her family: George, Zella, Bea and later Mary who had recently married Andy Skalkos from Hamilton. Zella, who was really pretty, was good friends with my cousin Mary and would visit us often. I really liked seeing her. She had a tremendous sense of humor to go along with her looks. I remember that when my uncle wanted to visit Thea Sophia for coffee, I was happy to go with him and enjoy Zella's great humor. She just made me laugh. Thea Sophia's son, George, and his cousins George Nick and George J. had formed a partnership in the ice cream business. They were making their own ice cream with the name brand "Elite" and selling it at their store on Central Avenue. Every time my uncle took me to the shop where the ice cream was made, one of the Georges would treat me to a cup of newly made ice cream. It was really delicious. I started to feel a little better and at ease with the people and my new surroundings. I cannot emphasize enough how nice people were to me.

Of all the people that I met on my first Sunday in Middletown and the days that followed, the ones to whom I related the most and with whom I later became good friends were Thea Frosine's boys: Mike, Chris, Charlie and later George, the older brother who was in Korea with the army, and Jim Demetrion. I cannot possibly express my appreciation for having such close and good friends as the above. I was and continue to be thankful and appreciative of my uncle and my cousins, but the above people, being closer to my age, made me feel as if I were one of their friends.

What can I say about Thea Frosine? She treated me like one of her sons when I was with them. I cannot say enough nice things about the Laras family, Paul Matthews, the Pantels, Hagias, the Uncle Jim and Uncle John Revelos families. They all played a role in my adjustment to being in America. When in Middletown during school breaks and vacations, I was invited along with my uncle for Thanksgiving and other holiday dinners at the Laras home, Uncle John's home and others. After church on Sundays, my uncle and I would join many friends at the Delicia Restaurant for lunch before going home.

During the first few Sundays that I was there, several of the people that I met at church came to visit us in the afternoon and brought Greek cookies and pastries with them. I remember sitting around the dining room table with everybody having coffee and pastries. Everyone was asking me all kinds of questions about Greece and particularly about what was happening in Vrontama because some of them were from there. I had the feeling that I impressed them with my knowledge not only of the news, but with the description of events that took place during the Greek civil war. Some of them had received the terrible letter that was sent to the Greek-Americans from Vrontama with the lies intended to discredit the pillars of the community, and they were asking me all kinds of questions relating to that letter.

I told them what the writers of that letter were doing during the occupation, which was cooperating with the enemy and spying against the Allies and the men fighting the enemy. They sent that letter because of jealousy and vindictiveness. I had lived in that period, and I felt that it was my duty to tell the truth and discredit the lowlife men in Vrontama who were responsible for the execution of ninety-four of its finest citizens by them and the outlaw gangs from Mani. I felt proud that I was given this opportunity to tell the truth and to dispel the lies that they had read in the letter. I described some of the events so graphically that some of the visitors had tears in their eyes, especially when I told the story of the teacher who was shot several times but still managed to crawl away. He was shot again. The village heard about it, and several people including his mother went to pick up the body. They found him still alive, and he died in the arms of his mother. All the people there were very happy to see me and hear the truth from someone who had experienced the war firsthand.

I believe that they all left my uncle's house with good impressions of me, and as I learned later, they compared the demeanor and knowledge of other young men coming from Greece to mine. One such young man who came from Greece at the invitation of his relatives was sent back to Greece because, they told my uncle, he was not as smart as his nephew. I never thought of myself as anything other than what I was. I was just a sixteen-year-old who came to America for medical treatment and who would return to Greece when I got well. I never thought of myself as someone who was better or worse than anyone. On the contrary, although I did not show it, I was scared in my new environment, but I always wore a smile and was pleasant to everyone. The Middletown people were very nice to me, especially Thea Frosine Revelos' sons and Jim Demetrion. My friendship with all of them has continued until now when we all have become senior citizens.

The Middletown Greek community was very close-knit, and the impression that I got was that they really cared about each other's families and the welfare of their local church. This was quite evident when they sponsored dinners and dances to raise money for their church. That really impressed me because in Greece the Greek Orthodox Church is a state church and the church's expenses are paid by the government, while here the Greek community has the total responsibility for the church's existence. I admired all the people who worked so hard in order to make sure that they had enough money to pay the priest and meet the other needs of their church.

As the days and weeks went by, I was getting to know more and more people and made friends with people of my age. One time I was invited to go to a high school football game in which Chris Revelos was playing. I went to the game with Jim Hagias and two others who came to my uncle's house to pick me up. I enjoyed the company but never understood the football game. I expected to see the football played in Europe, which here is called soccer, but I was watching something totally different and more complicated. I did not really understand football until I went to high school.

At times I felt very lonely and I missed the family atmosphere that I had in Greece. Thea Frosine and her sons always included me in the various social functions that they attended, but down deep I always felt like an outsider who was always introduced to others with the qualification of being George Manos' nephew from Greece instead of by my name alone. My uncle, Katherine, and Mary were always very nice to me, and I was grateful for everything that they did for me. Having Katherine and Mary in the house gave me a sense of security simply because of their presence in the house.

I met a man named Ted Sarris who had brothers in Vrontama who were good friends of our family. Ted and his wife happened to have two toddler boys, and my uncle convinced me to be the godfather of the youngest one. The other boy was to be baptized at the same time by his own godfather, who happened to be very old and an old-fashioned gentleman. Both boys were baptized at the same time, and when the time came to tell the priest the given names for the boys, I told the priest the name of my godson that the parents wanted, which was James. The other godfather named the child George when the priest asked for the child's name, while the parents wanted the name Steve. The parents got upset and told the priest that the name should be Steve. The godfather insisted on the name George. The priest, who also was from Greece, took the part of the godfather but gave the parents the option of giving the name Steve as a middle name. The christening proceeded without any other arguments, but the parents were quite unhappy about the whole thing. That other boy is still known as Steve.

My uncle, as I mentioned before, had pinball machines that he had placed in several restaurants and bars in Middletown and other cities in the area. Once each week he scheduled a visit to each of those places in order to empty the coin containers of each machine. He always asked me to go with him and help him count the nickels from the machines and place them in the $2 nickel wrappers. In order to count the nickels faster, he showed me how to count these coins two at a time and stack them up twenty in each stack. He introduced me everywhere we went as a newcomer from Greece and as his nephew. People started to know me as George Manos' nephew instead of by my own name. Actually, I could not blame my uncle for introducing me as his nephew because the name Karampas was not known in his business or in most of his social circles. What I missed was my family whom people knew and respected which would make it easier for my name to be remembered. It later became my goal that my name and my family's name would be known and remembered not only for my sake, but for the sake of my wife and my children.

I had been in Middletown for only two weeks when I answered the door bell and saw George Katsicopoulos, who had shortened his name to Pulos, and his sisters Mary and Joy at the door. I cannot describe my surprise and my happiness when I saw them. He was my good friend from Vrontama. I had skipped school to say goodbye to him when he and his family left for America. I had not seen them for more than four years. They were living in Dayton, Ohio which is only about twenty miles from Middletown. They came into my uncle's living room, and we started reminiscing about the times we had spent together in a village that was more than 5,000 miles away. When I told them that I never learned how to dance the Greek dances, they told me that they would teach me. My uncle had a good collection of Greek records and played them on the hi-fi. We all got up and they showed me the steps of some of the Greek dances. After a few times, I had learned enough to lead the dance. We spent several hours together and they left for Dayton at midnight. That was truly the highlight of my American experience up to that time. The Pulos family and I have never lost touch since that day. I treasure their friendship as I believe they treasure mine, and that friendship will last as long as we live.

A few days after I arrived in Middletown, my mother's brother Uncle Tony, his wife, Thea Alexandra, and my deceased Uncle George's wife, Aunt Mary, came to visit me from Valparaiso. I knew Uncle Tony and his wife from Greece where they got married about three and a half years before. I met Aunt Mary for the first time, and I was really impressed with her sense of humor and her wit. They spent a day with us and told us that my Uncle George's Forty Day Memorial was coming up shortly in Valparaiso and asked if we could attend the services. There was another member of the family that I had yet to meet; that was my mother's sister Thea Marigo who also had helped our family after the war. Uncle George asked me if I would like to go to Valparaiso for the memorial service, and of course, I said, "Yes." They also asked me to stay in Valparaiso for a few days and that Uncle Tony would bring me back when I wanted to return.

Going to Valparaiso

We left Middletown on the Friday before the Sunday of the memorial. My uncle was always a people-oriented person. When he traveled he wanted to have with him as much company as possible, so he asked Mrs. Hagias' cousin who was visiting from Greece to come along with me and my cousin Mary Kara. We stopped in Indianapolis for lunch, and from there we headed for Valparaiso where my Thea Marigo was expecting us.

As I mentioned previously, my aunt lost her husband about two months before she lost her brother, my Uncle George Lambros, who was actually the one who had invited me to come to America for medical treatment. Needless to say, my aunt was devastated with the loss of her husband and then her brother, and when she saw me she started to cry uncontrollably and told me that I reminded her of her brother. I then met Uncle Tony's sons, Elias (Louis) and his baby brother John, and my Uncle George's adopted son, Elias. Both Eliases were about three and a half years old, and John, only six months old.

We all visited and had dinner together at Thea Marigo's house. She asked me and Mary Kara to stay with her, while my Uncle George and the other man went to stay at my Aunt Mary Lambros' house. The next day we all got together at my Thea Marigo's house where we met the Kilavos family. Their son George later became one of my best friends. I met their daughter Lela at the memorial and the older brother, John, a year later when he returned from the navy.

Valparaiso did not have a Greek Orthodox Church, and we had to go to Gary, Indiana for the memorial. Gary is only twenty-five miles from Valparaiso, and the few Greek families that lived in Valparaiso went to the church in Gary. After church, we drove back to Valparaiso to my Uncle George's house where my Aunt Mary had the food catered while all the relatives who came brought cookies and pastries. Most of the people who came to the house came from Chicago, and almost all of them were related to me through my mother. I was really happy to meet everyone, and they all told me that they would like me to visit them in their home when someone could take me there.

With help from Thea Marigo, Uncle Tony had bought the only pool hall in Valparaiso. It had ten pool tables in a long, narrow room with chairs for people to sit while waiting for their turn to play. At the far end of the billiard room was a closed-in area where some of the men would go to play poker for money. Of course, gambling was illegal, but the people who went to that room to play were mostly prominent people in the city. I even saw the chief of police and the mayor himself going in the back to play poker. On Saturday nights, Uncle Tony would bring in food for all the poker players.

Uncle Tony had rented a small house in the city where Thea Alexandra took care of their two sons. He had come to America from Australia via Greece in 1947, and after some unsuccessful business ventures, he settled in Valparaiso. Although his two sons had been born in the United States, he was still considered an alien. It took several years to settle this matter with the Immigration and Naturalization Service. Although he was Thea Marigo's brother, she had lost confidence in him because of his unsuccessful business ventures and because he was constantly asking her for money to support his family. Thea Marigo would sit down with me and tell me these things. I was the only one in whom she would confide family matters.

The day after the memorial service, my uncle and the others returned to Middletown, but I stayed in Valparaiso for a while to keep my Thea Marigo company. On Monday, Thea Marigo gave money to Aunt Mary to take me to a store and buy me a suit, new shirts, ties and shoes. Until that time, I had been wearing the same suit with which I had come to America. I liked everything that my aunt bought me.

I stayed in Valparaiso for three weeks during which I met all the Greek people in town. George Kilavos, who had a really old car, took me to a high school game and other places in the city such as Valparaiso University and the Rec Room where many kids of my age would congregate to play pool and listen to music.

The reason for my short stay in Valparaiso was that Uncle George Manos wanted to enroll me in Middletown High School, so when my time came up, Uncle Tony drove me back to Middletown. When I returned to Middletown, things had changed somewhat.

Deciding to Live in Valparaiso

When I returned to Middletown, my cousin Katherine had decided to go live in New York with her brother Peter. Mary, at that time, was working in Middletown, and except for the weekends, she was not home. Many times that left me alone at my uncle's home because my uncle would be out visiting people or going to the restaurants or bars to empty the cash boxes of the pinball machines. Most of the time he took me with him, and I really enjoyed going to all those places, but there was something missing in all that. It was the absence of some kind of order in my life. My uncle had been a bachelor all his life, and although it was not his fault, he was not able to understand the thinking of a sixteen-year-old.

There were lots of positive things that I really liked in Middletown: the friends that I had made in the short time that I was there, the families that I had met, and yes, my uncle and my cousin Mary, who had done everything to make me feel welcome. However, when I was in Valparaiso, it felt more like home, more of a family and orderly environment with my Thea Marigo. I also had become good friends with George Kilavos and other families in town which would make it easier for me to adjust to living in Valparaiso. The overriding factor, however, was that I felt sorry for my aunt who was left alone to grieve after the death of her husband and her brother. Although my Uncle Tony was there, he had to deal with his work and a growing family. In 1952, a beautiful little girl named Margarita joined her brothers. Uncle Tony's billiard business was not going well, so he and his family decided to move to Hammond, Indiana where he went into the restaurant business.

Before I left Valparaiso to return to Middletown, Thea Marigo had asked me with tears in her eyes to come back and stay with her. That picture played a major role in my decision. I was faced with the decision of where I wanted to live. It was a difficult decision because I would have been happy in both places. I decided to go live with my Thea Marigo because I was needed there more than in Middletown.

In fear of appearing ungrateful for everything that my uncle and cousin Mary had done for me and not wanting to upset them, I wrote a letter to my father and asked him to write a letter to my uncle recommending that it would be helpful to my Thea Marigo if I were to go live with her. It may have seemed that I was suggesting this strictly for selfish reasons, but in my heart I really felt sorry for my aunt and I thought it would make her pain a little less if she had me in her home. Looking back, I made the right decision.

A few weeks later, my uncle received a letter from my father explaining to him the reasons for which it would be better for me to go live with my Thea Marigo in Valparaiso. My uncle told me of my father's letter and asked me if I agreed with what he had written. Actually, my uncle seemed somewhat relieved when I agreed with my father, which made me feel a little better about leaving him and my cousin Mary. Both of them told me that they wanted me to think of Middletown as my home and that I should come there for holidays and summer vacations.

And so, my uncle and Mary Kara drove me to Valparaiso where I stayed with my aunt for approximately seven years. My aunt was very happy to see me come back, and from then on she always treated me with the love of a mother. After a few weeks, Mary took a job in Chicago, and my uncle was left alone in the house again. Although my permanent home was in Valparaiso, I went to Middletown on every occasion that I could. That gave me the opportunity to meet with my Middletown friends and keep our friendships strong.

Going to Valparaiso High School

The Monday after I came back to Valparaiso, my Uncle Tony took me to Valparaiso High School to meet the principal and to decide what courses I should take. They explained to me that the courses that I would be taking were English, woodworking, gym, and others. Since my English was very limited at that time, I really did not know what all those courses were. George Kilavos was asked to come to the principal's office where he was briefed on my curriculum. He reassured me that I should not be worried because for the first few days, he would take me to the classes that I needed to attend. They assigned me a locker and gave me the key. George explained to me the purpose of the locker: that I was supposed to hang my coat there in the morning and keep the books that I needed going from one class to another. George had an old car, and he told me that he would pick me up and give me a ride to and from school every day. The next day he came and picked me up for school.

George was a very popular young man and a track star who held school records in several events. He had a great sense of humor and would go out of his way to help anyone who needed his help. When he pulled up in front of my aunt's house to pick me up, he opened one of the two car doors and I saw three other people in it. It was a small car and I wondered how we could all fit in it. Somehow, we all squeezed into the jalopy, and I went to an American school for the first time. George took me to my first class and introduced me to my English teacher. She also taught French and asked me if I could speak that language. Although not very fond of French, I told her that I knew a little. She showed me my seat in the classroom and asked me to stand up while she introduced me to the other students. It so happened that a second cousin of mine was in the same class. I had met her in her family home and tried to talk to her, but she gave me the impression that she wanted to keep her distance from me and did not want to have anything to do with me, especially in school. I got the message quickly and except for the "hello" greeting, we acted like complete strangers.

We had about ten minutes between classes, and during that time, the students would walk around the hallways and talk to their friends. Since I was a complete stranger, I would stand in front of a window by the entrance to the school and wait for my next class. I was really surprised when several students came to me, telling me that they wanted to be friends with me. Little by little, I learned quite a bit of English from the students who came to talk to me. What impressed me was that none of them made fun of me and my broken English. As frightened as I was at times when the teachers asked me questions that I was not able to answer well in English, I had developed a positive attitude about school and everyone around me.

During my childhood, because of the war, living with my aunt in Kosma during the summers, and being mindful of the danger of losing our lives during the Greek civil war, I had learned to cope and get along in all kinds of environments and situations. I started to consider every new experience in America as a challenge and became determined to learn from everyone around me. I was and still am a people person and always want to be around others from whom I can learn and with whom I could become friends. Other students responded to my need of asking questions about English, spelling, or sports. This helped me to become a better student and most of all a better human being and a better American.

One of my favorite classes was the woodworking class. After the initial introduction to how everything worked, I was to choose something that I wanted to make out of wood. I found a drawing of a wooden bowl with a nut cracker in the middle. This drew my interest because it was something that I could make and send to my parents in Greece as a gift from me. I learned how to work with the lathe machine and within two weeks, I had it completed. The teacher, Mr. Pfeifer, gave me an "A" for this project. Mr. Pfeifer was also the coach for the track team, and the following year he asked me if I wanted to join the team. I told him that in the summer I was supposed to have an operation on my leg and that I would like to be on his team when the doctor gave me his permission.

The following year I joined the track team and I ran the 100 yard dash, the 220 yard run and the half-mile relay. I only won a few races in competition, but I earned the letter 'V' that I wore on my jacket with pride. Although I was not aware at that time, my right leg was longer than the left because after my operation in 1941, the right leg had been placed in traction which made it a little longer than the left leg. I believe that if it were not for this disparity, I would have been a much better runner and would have won many more races. Besides track, I went to the high school gym on a regular basis in the evenings after completing my homework and joined other high school kids playing basketball and working out. I did all of the above not only because I enjoyed the physical exercise, but also because socializing with other students helped me become more proficient in English.

One day when I was in my ninth grade English class, the school principal Mr. King Telle came to class and asked me to go with him. He took me to his car and we both went to the Lemke Hotel in the center of Valparaiso. He led me to the dining room that was full of business men sitting around the tables having lunch. I did not have the faintest idea what to expect. At that time, I had been in school for only three months. With some apprehension, I sat next to Mr. Telle and soon they brought our lunch. Mr. Telle then told me that I was to speak in front of all these people, about fifty to sixty of them, and tell them about my experiences in Greece and America. At that time Valparaiso was a small town of about 17,000 people. There were not many visitors from other countries. Even a teenage boy with a limited understanding of English could provide interesting information. Needless to say, I had never spoken to any large-sized group before, especially such older gentlemen and in such a setting. After eating lunch, Mr. Telle got up and introduced me to the members of the Valparaiso Rotary Club. Everyone applauded, and shaking a little, I stood up and in broken English I told them that I had come from Greece the prior September and I now lived with my Thea Marigo at 103 Indiana Avenue in Valparaiso. Everyone seemed to be listening intently to what I had to say which gave me the courage to ask them for any questions that they wanted to ask me. I stood and answered many of their questions, as best as I could, for almost forty-five minutes. I thanked them for my lunch and returned to school with Mr. Telle, who was always nice to me whenever he saw me in school or on the street. From then on, most of the business people in Valparaiso knew me by name, and every time I passed by their office or their store, they would always greet me or wave to me. I was finally my own person, not just someone's nephew from Greece.

In the evenings and on weekends my primary activity was studying in order to catch up with the other students. My Greek-American dictionary was my constant companion in school and at home. I was struggling to understand what I was reading, but I was determined to become proficient in English and not have to use the dictionary as much. Once in a while George Kilavos and I would go to a movie or to one of several root beer stands in town. This was a great gesture by George, and I always expressed my appreciation to him by helping him wash his car.

My aunt did not have a television at that time, and there was not much to do around the house. Uncle Tony would come and ask me if I wanted to go to his pool hall and help him. Naturally, I always went when he asked me. My job was to rack the billiard balls at the end of each game and collect the money from the customers. I also served as the cashier for the customers who were buying soft drinks from the cooler and magazines from the racks. Uncle Tony spent most of his time in the back room with the poker players. He never offered and I never asked to be paid for the work that I was doing. I considered that work as part of my American education. I was learning English from everybody, and I always performed my job with a smile, which made everyone want to help me.

My curriculum for my second year included courses in civics and geometry. I really got to love those two courses and I excelled in both of them. In Civics I learned how this country works and the responsibilities of each of the three branches of government. In Geometry, I was one of the best students in the class. There was only one problem. I had a severe case of nearsightedness, and I was not always able to see other students' work on the board. The teacher noticed that I was squinting a lot and told me to see a doctor for glasses. I told my aunt about this, and the next day she took me to an optometrist who checked my eyes and sold us a pair of glasses. When I wore them for the first time in school, I was so happy to be able to read things written on the blackboards even when I sat in the back of the classroom.

I started to enjoy my stay in America and my initial homesickness was fading away. Although I started being comfortable in America, I never forgot my father's advice when I left Greece. I communicated with my parents and most of my relatives by mail at least once a week and kept them current about all my activities. My parents were proud and grateful that I had become such a good and descriptive correspondent. My correspondence with my parents on a weekly basis lasted until well after I was married and had children. Eventually I wrote to my parents less frequently and communicated with them by telephone, which had become more convenient.

Immigration Problems

On my first visit to Valparaiso, my Uncle Tony had taken me to a doctor in Michigan City, Indiana to have my leg examined. The doctor told him that I needed to go to a clinic for treatment. My uncles decided to wait until the end of the school year to take me for further examinations. Then I would have the summer to recuperate from an operation and not miss any school.

In May 1951 my Uncle George took me to the Mayo Clinic in Rochester, Minnesota to have my leg problem diagnosed and cured. The doctors recommended that I should have an operation at the clinic, which would keep me in Rochester for almost a month. Since it was impossible for my uncle to stay with me there during that time, he decided to take me back to Valparaiso and have the operation in a Chicago hospital. A relative who was a registered nurse worked at the University of Chicago Hospital and recommended a good surgeon to perform the operation on me. And so it was. I had the operation on my right leg in the summer of 1951, and after staying in the hospital for ten days, I was released and returned to Valparaiso. The operation was successful, but I had to walk on crutches for a month. I had lost a lot of weight and was down to the level that I was when I came from Greece. By the end of the summer, I was ready to return to Valparaiso High School and continue my education.

It was October and Homecoming was to take place the following Friday. Everyone was looking forward to the football game and then taking their dates to Browny's, a teen hangout, for a hamburger and a milkshake. Then there was a dance that everyone could attend. I mustered enough courage to ask a sophomore girl named Carol Black to go to the Homecoming events with me. This was the first time that I had asked a girl for a date, and I was scared that she would say "no." To my surprise, she said that she would go to the activities after the ballgame with me. She was a cheerleader and was not able to sit with me during the game. I ordered a corsage, but not having a car, I asked one of my friends who had one if we could double date. I was looking forward to Friday until everything changed.

My Uncle George Manos was paying a woman in Chicago to find a way for me to stay in America permanently because up to this time I was here on a medical visa. Now that I had had the operation, according to the law, I should have returned to Greece. She kept telling us that she was close to changing my immigration status from medical treatment to that of a permanent resident. Well, that never happened, even though my uncle kept paying her for that purpose.

In October 1952 two INS agents came to school and told me that I was staying in America illegally and that I had to go with them. My Thea Marigo had gone to Greece for two months, and I was living in her home alone except for Uncle Tony and his family who lived in an apartment in the same building. The INS agents were taking me away in their car when I asked them to at least let me tell Thea Alexandra that I was going with them. They agreed, and I asked Thea Alexandra to get in touch with my uncle from Middletown and tell him what was happening.

I was taken to the Lake County Jail in Crown Point, Indiana where I was booked, fingerprinted and put in jail. Later I learned that this was the jail where a notorious gangster named John Dillinger had been kept, but he escaped from it only to be found later killed outside of a Chicago theater. The part of the jail where I was taken had open cells with only iron bars separating them and a cell door without a key. The cells were around an open area where the inmates could sit and play checkers or other board games. I was really scared and did not have the faintest idea what was going to happen to me. I spent all my time sitting in one of the cells alone because a couple of the inmates had gotten into a fight and had to be separated by the guard. I could see from the small high windows that it was getting dark outside. A little later, the lights were turned off, and full darkness prevailed which added to my anxiety. That is when I was even more scared. I lay on the hanging bed and hoped to go to sleep quickly. They had given me a light blanket, but it was not enough to keep me warm. I used it to cover my head to avoid seeing what everyone was doing. There I was in jail when I could have been watching my school's homecoming game and my date cheering our team to victory.

I saw the rays of the sun coming in from the small windows and said a short prayer thanking God that I was okay. At about noon, a guard came and took me to an office where the same two men who had taken me from school the day before were waiting. They took me to their car and then to the INS office in Gary, Indiana where they told me that my uncle had put up the bond for my release. They gave me a paper stating that I had to leave America in fifteen days. If I did not leave, I would be arrested again and put in jail for much longer than one day. Uncle Tony was there and he drove me to Valparaiso. The next day I went back to school and many of my fellow students came over to greet me. My Uncle George came to see me and gave me an airline ticket to and from Greece. He advised me that when I returned to Greece, I should go to the United States Embassy and apply for a student visa.

In the meantime, my class in school had a meeting and decided to give me our class ring as a gift from all of them. That ring was presented to me at a class convocation which was attended by my classmates. I was so overcome with emotion from the students' kindness and generosity that I broke down crying while everyone was clapping their hands. I was speechless and the only thing that I was able to say was "thank you." Later I told some of my closest friends who came to talk to me personally that I was going to try to return and continue my education in Valparaiso. Thea Marigo returned from Greece five days before I had to leave the country and kept asking if there was anything that she could do to keep me from being deported. There was nothing that anyone could do at that point.

On November 13, 1952 I went to Chicago and from there to Athens where my parents were waiting for me. We had not seen each other for a little over two years, and it was a very emotional reunion. In 1950, I had left from our one-room apartment in Sepolia; now my father had started to build on the lot that he had purchased before I left Greece. As incomplete as it was, my family had moved into their new house in the area called "Neos Cosmos." The house had one big room, a kitchen, and a bathroom. The floors were not finished and were made out of dirt. I shared my parents' and my sister's joy in finally having a place of their own. The next day my parents asked me if I really wanted to go back to America or stay there with my family and return to my old high school in Athens.

I found myself in the middle of a crossroad, making a decision that would affect me for the rest of my life. I started to evaluate my situation in America and in Greece. If I decided to stay in Greece and went back to my old school, I would have to start over again to make up the classes that I had missed for two years. And what was to happen to me after graduation? Would I be able to go to college? At that time it was very difficult to get into any university in Greece. At least for a while, although my parents would not think of it this way, I would become a burden to the limited resources of my family. Besides, I had started to like living in America. Upon finishing high school, I would be able to go to Valparaiso University and find summer jobs and part-time jobs during school to pay for most of my expenses. After thinking for a while, I told my father and mother of my decision to go back to America, explaining to them my reasons for it and also promising them that I would reconsider returning to Greece after I received my degree from Valparaiso University. That seemed to sooth my mother's pain a little at my leaving.

My father and I went to the American Embassy the next day, and I applied for re-entry to the United States, this time as a student. Within two days my paperwork was finished and my return to America was set for December 15, 1952. Before I left Greece again, I wanted to visit my village Vrontama that I loved so much and had not seen for over two years. There I visited with my Uncle John, my friend and relative Demetri

Koutsovasiles, and my cousin George Tsuturas, who came to see me from Zoupaina. I gave him a suit that my aunt had bought for me in Valparaiso which had become a little too small for me. Three years later Demetri went to live and work in Australia, and I did not see him again for over thirty-five years, until the summer of 1988. George Tsuturas was invited by my uncle in Middletown and came to the United States as a permanent resident in the spring of 1955.

I returned to Athens and on December 15, I flew with TWA to New York and then to Chicago. Once again we said our tearful goodbyes, but this time I knew where I was going and what to expect. This made it easier for me to leave, but it did not comfort my parents who gave me their blessing before I got on the plane. Now I was safe from being deported again as long as I was going to school.

Back in Valparaiso

I returned to my classes at Valparaiso High School, and many students came to greet me and ask me questions about why I had had to leave. A reporter from the Vidette Messenger, the Valparaiso newspaper, came to school and told me that he wanted to do a story about me in his newspaper. He asked me for a picture, and I gave him one taken in front of the TWA plane before leaving Chicago for Greece. The next day I saw the story on the front page of the paper under the heading "Deported VHS Student Returns." The school paper also did a similar article upon my return.

While I was in Greece, I went to my old high school in Athens and got a list of courses and grades that I had before leaving for America. I took it to the high school counselor who looked at the list of courses and decided that I was more advanced than the students in the class in which the school had put me initially. This made me eligible to graduate at the end of the 1953 school year. I continued to study hard, especially English. By this time, the time that I spent studying English by looking up words in the English-Greek dictionary was reduced considerably, but not totally. I was doing well in school, but I really had to work hard at it. Many evenings I went to work in my uncle's pool hall. On the weekends, I attended all the sport events of my school. I was always invited to go to school dances that any student could attend by paying twenty-five cents. The money paid for the music that was provided by the student band.

In the spring of 1953, the track coach asked me again if I wanted to join his team and I did. I had the fundamentals and the good speed to run the 100 and 220-yard dashes and the half-mile relay. I won a few events, but I experienced a swelling above the knee of my right leg and had to quit after I had enough credits to receive the school letter.

In May of that year, I attended my first prom. I asked one of my classmates named Ingrid, a girl who came from Austria, to go with me and she accepted. We double-dated with a friend of mine, and after the dance, we all went to a restaurant for dinner. The next day, my friend and I picked up our dates from the prom and went to the "Dunes" at Lake Michigan for swimming. We all had a great time that weekend which was the end of my high school life and the beginning of my working and college life.

Before graduation, Mr. Telle's secretary called me to the office and asked me if I had a summer job. Since I did not have a job lined up, she called the Personnel Department of the Indiana Steel Products Company in Valparaiso and scheduled an interview for me. Naturally I went and was told that I should report for work in a week. Graduation was on June 11, 1953, and my Thea Marigo, Uncle Tony's family, and Uncle George from Middletown were there for me.

In a week I started working in the plant that produced magnets of all sizes and shapes. I was told that most of the magnets made there were used by the fighter jet manufacturers for the airplanes they were making for the government. Every jet in those days needed at least one hundred magnets of various sizes and shapes in order to be operational. America, at that time, was engaged in the Korean War, and we were reminded that the quality of our work was very important. On my first day, the foreman took me to my work station. My job was to make the forms that would receive the melted steel to make the magnets. It turned out that it was one of the toughest jobs in the plant. The people next to me had been doing the same job for many years, and they were much older, bigger and more rugged than I was. The job required lifting sixty to seventy pounds many times a day, which was taking a toll on my back. My hourly pay was $2.05, and a month later they raised it to $2.27. Those amounts were increased by half every time I was asked to work overtime, which was at least once a week. Payday was my favorite day because after work I went to the bank, kept a small amount from my check, and deposited the rest in my checking account. During that summer, I really did not need much money because I was working so hard that at the end of my shift I was too tired to do anything else but stay home and study to prepare myself for going to college in the fall. At the end of the summer I had about $600 in the bank and thought I was rich.

My aunt did not have a car and did not even know how to drive which was why I took a driving class in my last year of high school. The closest Greek Orthodox Church to us was in Gary, Indiana, about twenty-seven miles from home. My aunt and I always wanted to go to church, but we had to depend on my Uncle Tony or others to take us there. My Uncle Tony and Thea Alexandra had three children at the time, and he was not always able to take us. After discussing the situation, my aunt and I decided that I should buy an old car that we could use for going to church, to the grocery, and to and from my classes when college started. I asked my friend George Kilavos to help me look for a car, and with his help, I found a 1942 Plymouth that I was able to buy for $225. That left me with $375 in the bank because my aunt paid for the car insurance. She and my uncle from Middletown told me that they were going to pay for my tuition which was $450 for the year. They also told me to use the money that I had in the bank for my books and for transportation to and from Middletown whenever I decided to go and visit my uncle and my Middletown friends.

Going to College

I decided to attend Valparaiso University so that I could commute to my classes from my aunt's house. By doing that, I could save money and keep my aunt company. My first year of college was quite difficult because I had to read books with the help of my constant companion, the English-Greek Dictionary. Also, thinking that I would return to Greece after college, I enrolled in the College of Engineering. That was a calculated move on my part because if I returned to Greece with a degree in engineering, I would be able to find a job immediately. I found out that I was not cut out to be an engineer because I did not possess the needed discipline, and my grades showed it by the end of my first year. I made the decision with my advisor that in the fall I would enroll in the College of Business.

During my summer break of 1954, I was not able to find a job in Valparaiso, and my uncle told me that if I came to Middletown, I would find a summer job quickly. So I did go to Middletown, and I got a job with The Ohio Ice Cream Company from Hamilton, Ohio. My job was to drive a small truck and sell ice cream and ice cream novelties in several neighborhoods in Cincinnati.

At that time most homes did not have air conditioning, and in the afternoons and evenings people would sit outside, which made it easy for me to sell ice cream, especially to the children. I rented a room in a house in Norwood and stayed there at night. I started working at 10:00 in the morning and did not return to my room until midnight. I worked really hard, and by the company's standards, I was the best salesman they had. When I received my first check, it was for less than $90 out of which I had to pay for my room and my food, leaving me with about $50 per week to save for my next year in college. I talked to my boss who encouraged me to stay on saying that things would get better. My pay was mostly dependent on sales. Although I kept working long, hard hours, things were not getting any better, and after three weeks, I told the company that I was quitting.

I returned to Valparaiso where Uncle Tony asked me to work for him at a restaurant named "Snack Bar" in Chicago Heights, Illinois. His business at the pool hall he had in Valparaiso was not producing the income he needed to support his family. He had moved from Valparaiso and was living in Hammond, Indiana because he wanted his family to be able to live in a community that had a Greek Orthodox Church and also because his new home was closer to his new business. This job made it necessary for me to rent a room close to the restaurant. My job was to be the cashier and help with the washing of dishes and the cleaning of the restaurant after closing. I started working at 8:00 in the morning, had two hours off in the afternoon, and returned to work until 9:00 in the evening when the store closed. I worked at the restaurant for three weeks and my uncle had not paid me. I told him that I needed to pay for my room, and he gave me enough cash to pay the landlord for one month.

We were closed on Sundays which gave me the opportunity to go to Valparaiso, see my aunt, and go to church. She asked me how much her brother was paying me. When I told her that I did not know, she got really mad at him, and the next time she saw him, she read the riot act to him for taking advantage of his sister's son. For the two and a half months that I worked for him, he paid me $250 plus my room rent of $50. After that I made up my mind that I would never work for a relative again.

The fall semester of college started in the middle of September, and I enrolled in the College of Business. I started doing much better that year, and I liked it much more as time went by.

One of the members of the Board of Directors of the University from Houston, Texas had a plant in Valparaiso where he employed students from the university on a part-time basis. The plant made all kinds of outdoor furniture out of cedar wood. I applied for a part-time job in that company named "Branco Corporation of Indiana" and worked about twenty to thirty hours a week. I was careful not to work at the expense of my classes. I was getting paid $1.25 an hour which was enough to pay for my gas, going to the movies, and later, my fraternity dues.

For the rest of my college career, I did very well in all my classes, and for four semesters I made the Dean's List. In the summers I found work in Gary, Indiana and worked at the Gary Works of US Steel. I also worked for Inland Steel in East Chicago. All the summer jobs that I had were hard and dirty, but I was paid well for a college student.

George Kilavos was also going to VU, but he was two years ahead of me. He used to take me to the Theta Chi Fraternity house where he was a member and introduced me to several of his fraternity brothers. I got to know many of them well, and in my second year I was asked to join Theta Chi. It was the tradition in the fraternity, and I imagine in all men's fraternities, that the day before the actual initiation, during which a pledge would become a full member, he would go through a "Hell Night." Each pledge went through a pre-initiation hazing which was much worse than anything that happened during the pledge period that usually lasted for one to two months.

On that dreadful day for everyone in the fall pledge class, after some demeaning activities for all of us, each pledge was put into a car, blindfolded, and driven to an unknown destination. What made it worse was that the weather was terrible by any standards. That day it started snowing in the afternoon and continued to snow during the entire night. I was driven blindfolded for about one hour, and all I could hear was the conversation from the front seat between two active members of the fraternity who were making comments to scare me. After an hour, the car stopped and the door opened. I was asked to get out of the car and wait for five minutes before removing the blindfold. When I took the blindfold off after a couple minutes, I found myself in the middle of nowhere, and it was snowing heavily. I started walking following the tracks of the car that left me there, but after a while they were covered with new snow and I was on my own.

I had walked for about 400 yards when I saw the lights of a car coming from behind me. The car stopped when they saw me in the middle of the road. I went by the driver's side, and I saw an old man and his wife. I didn't know where I was, so I asked them where they were going. They were going to a small town named Hebron, about fifteen miles from Valparaiso. I asked them to give me a ride to Hebron. They told me that they were coming back from a party in the country, and it did not take me long to see that they were both very drunk because the man was driving toward the river that was on the side of that road. I yelled for him to stop the car, but the car was sliding toward the river. I reached for the steering wheel from the back seat and turned the car to the opposite direction. The car finally stopped, and I asked the man if I could do the rest of the driving for him. Surprisingly, he agreed and following his directions, we arrived at Hebron. I got out of the car and went straight to a small building with two police cars in front of it. That was the police station, and I asked a policeman if I could sleep in jail until morning. He asked me what crime I had committed. When I told him that I had not done anything against the law, he told me that the jail was only for criminals and asked me to leave the station.

I walked a block toward the road to Valparaiso, and on my right I saw a two-story house with a porch in front of it. I walked to the door and knocked a couple times, but there was no answer. I pried the door a little and it opened. I got inside the house, and without making any noise, I sat on the floor and leaned against an old radiator that was on the right side of a small hall with stairs leading to the second floor. The heat from the radiator felt really good since I was freezing and I fell asleep. The next thing I knew, I was awakened by an old man who wanted to know what I was doing in his house. After I told him my story, he asked me if I was hungry and invited me to have breakfast with his wife. I left thanking them both and walked out to see if I could find a ride by hitchhiking. The fraternity's Fall Formal was that night, and I did not want to miss it and disappoint my date. A pick-up truck picked me up and took me to the fraternity house where I had left my car. I was informed that I was the last to come in from "Hell Night." I drove home, picked up my tuxedo and the corsage for my date, and after cleaning up and getting some sleep, I was ready for the evening's events.

The next day I was initiated. I was so proud to wear my red jacket with the letters Theta Chi on the front. As it turned out, that was one of the best decisions that I could have made at the time. I learned how to get along with all my fraternity brothers who always made themselves available to me during my Americanization process, including teaching me parliamentary procedure at meetings. I will always be grateful to my friend George Kilavos who introduced me to the Theta Chi Fraternity.

After I became a member of the fraternity, I became each pledge class's biggest challenge, especially during hazing and weekly pledge meetings. At each meeting, each pledge had to race me in saying the Greek alphabet as fast as he could. Naturally, although they all knew the alphabet, they were no match for me in saying it fast. I always said it faster than anyone, and at times I showed off a little by skipping some of the letters without anyone noticing.

One day in the fall of 1954, a delivery truck hit a front fender of my car outside of the fraternity house. Since I did not see who hit my car to ask for payment for the damages, I decided to knock the damaged fender out with a hammer and then paint it myself the same color as the rest of the car. Or so I thought! Hitting the fender with a hammer was cost effective, but the hammer left hammer marks all over the fender and the original paint was totally damaged. I went and bought some paint to match the original paint of the car which was light brown. I started to apply the paint on the fender with a brush when I noticed that the new paint was gold and not brown. The car was old, but as long as I was able to drive it safely, there was no harm done. I finished painting the damaged fender with the gold paint. After looking at my car for a while, I noticed that the gold on the fender and the brown on the rest of the car were the colors of Valparaiso University. I then decided to paint the other three fenders gold which would make the car look a little more balanced and it did. After that I was asked to drive my brown and gold car in the Homecoming Parades, with some of the cheerleaders hanging out of the windows with their pompoms.

From then on my car was recognized by everyone on campus, and the students waived at me every time they saw me. I kept that car until the fall of 1956 at which time one of the fraternity brothers made me an offer that I could not refuse. He paid me $175 and drove it to his home in Pennsylvania and back for Thanksgiving and Christmas, and it was still running well. With money from my part-time work, I bought a 1956 Dodge.

Most of the time, the men of Theta Chi were a very cohesive group. We went to the ballgames together, and we generally hung around the fraternity house playing cards, watching television and even enjoying our own beer parties, which at times got a little sloppy. The members were able to bring their dates into the house during the weekends to watch TV. All the members had to be on their best behavior. I really enjoyed my college years in Valparaiso from where I graduated in January 1958 with many good memories and experiences.

Friendships in Valparaiso

In 1955 Jim Kilavos, his wife Mary (Katsicopoulos) and their son George moved to Valparaiso from Dayton in search of a better job. Jim was a good car mechanic and started to work for a Buick dealer in town. Jim and George Katsicopoulos had been good friends in our village in Greece. Jim and Mary had fallen in love before Mary came to America, and in 1951 she went back to Greece and married him. A few months later, Jim joined Mary in Dayton and soon their first child, George, was born. Now that they were in Valparaiso, we continued our friendship, and that gave me the opportunity to be able to connect with my life in Greece. We would see each other often, and we became even better friends. My Thea Marigo was Mary's godmother. Mary was baptized by my aunt in America before the Katsicopoulos family moved to Greece in the thirties.

In the summer of 1955, before my summer job started, George Kilavos and his mother invited me to join them on a trip to Fernandina Beach, Florida where they were going to a baptism. They asked me if I wanted to go with them as a vacation. I jumped at that chance because I had never been to Florida and I thought that we would have a great time driving to Florida and back. I saw it as an opportunity to see several other states along the way.

The people they were visiting had us stay in their beach house, and we were able to go swimming anytime we wanted. The family would come after dark to catch fish by taking a net into the ocean for fifty to one hundred feet and then dragging it back to the beach. Naturally, George and I helped them by taking the net into the ocean while they would hold the other end of the net. Because the net would get heavy from the fish caught in it, everyone would come in to help. Surprisingly, we caught many fish of all sizes and many crabs. We would let the crabs go back in the ocean while the fish were separated by type and dropped into plastic containers for the market. We were asked to keep as many of the fish as we wanted, and Thea Kondilo would cook them for all of us. George and I visited St. Augustine, Jacksonville and other smaller cities in the area. We all had a very good time, and I was thankful to George and his mother for asking me to go with them on that trip.

George's brother, John Kilavos, who was in the navy when I first went to Valparaiso, came back in 1951. In the spring of 1952 George's and John's father died, and John had to take over his restaurant to support the family. George worked there during his off-school hours and so did Thea Kondilo. Their sister Lela was going to graduate school for her Master's in Education and did not work. In the mid-fifties, John met his future wife Penny Anast from Chicago. He asked me to be the best man at his wedding and naturally I accepted. Everyone from Valparaiso was invited. Being the koumbaro, I was asked if I wanted to invite anyone to the wedding, and an invitation was sent to my uncle in Middletown. By that time, my cousin George Tsuturas had come from Greece to live in Middletown with my uncle, and an invitation was extended to him as well. In fact, I asked George to be the assistant koumbaro and he accepted.

The wedding took place in a church in Chicago, and it was followed by a big reception with live Greek-American music. Thea Marigo was very proud of me for carrying out my duties as a koumbaro so well. At the reception, my uncle kept introducing me to some eligible girls telling me that when college was over, I would have to leave the country unless I found someone to marry me. Although I still had almost three years of college left, he was always saying, "You have to start cooking before you get hungry." A year later John and Penny had their first son, and they asked me to be his godfather. The baptism was in Chicago and the baby was named Thomas after his grandfather. I had become very good friends with the entire Kilavos family, and we all took turns having dinner together at my aunt's and Thea Kondilo's house.

Although I lived in Valparaiso through college, I never forgot my uncle and the friends that I had made in Middletown. I went to Middletown every chance I had, and I kept my friendships strong during my college years. On holidays such as Easter, Mother's Day and Memorial Day, I went to Middletown to help my uncle sell flowers. He would rent an empty store in downtown Middletown and sell flowers that he bought wholesale from greenhouses in nearby cities. We would rent a truck, and I would drive it to the greenhouses, load it with potted flowers, drive back to Middletown, unload the truck and get the flowers ready for display. In addition to my help, my uncle would ask anyone who was available to help with the sale. I did not mind helping my uncle at all because I felt that I owed him a lot for what he had done for me, plus I learned something about flowers. After the last day of business, I would drive back to Valparaiso where I would attend classes the next day.

Biggest Decision of My Life

After my January graduation from college, the time that I dreaded the most had arrived. I had to make the decision whether I wanted to stay in America permanently or return to Greece to an insecure future and perhaps become a liability to my family that was already struggling financially. When I first left Greece, I always thought that I would be returning home after my leg was healed. I thought that when I was older I would be supportive of my aging parents and my sister. Life, however, has a way of presenting us choices that, for better or worse, can change the path we thought we would take.

During my high school and college years, I began to look at America as a country that I could make my home because of the freedoms that Americans enjoy and the opportunities that hard work can present. I was also impressed with the genuine friendliness and eagerness to help of the American people. I believed that I could make a better life for myself in America than in Greece and that I would also be able to help my family financially. I wasn't sure that I would be able to help them if I went back to Greece. After weighing all my options, I decided that I would stay and make a life for myself in America. When I told my parents of my decision, they were not surprised. My parents never objected to me making my own decisions. They just wanted me to be sure that living in America was what I really wanted to do. They said that they would support me no matter what I decided. It was a difficult decision for me to make because I always felt very close to my family in Greece even though I had been away from them for several years. I knew that I would miss my family, my relatives and my friends, and they, in return, would miss me, too.

My anxiety at being in America was gone, but my guilt for leaving my family would never go away. It has stayed with me, in various degrees, all my life and has influenced some of my decisions. My weekly correspondence with my parents until their death did make me feel as though I were still a member of my family in Greece and took away some of my guilt, but I still felt that I had abandoned them in some way.

The question, however, that kept coming to my mind was "How can I stay in America when I am here on a student visa?" My only choice at the time was to marry a citizen of the United States. I was not financially or emotionally ready to marry anyone at that time. Even if I were, I did not know anyone who would marry me. I always wanted to marry a Greek-American girl because I treasure our religion and all the customs that made me the person that I am. I had no name recognition in America, and the girls in whom I might have been interested at the time were not attracted to me because they did not know anything about me, my background, or my family.

My uncle kept introducing me to a few girls, but neither I nor any of the girls had any interest in each other. My uncle then made the following suggestion to me. A marriage could be arranged with a girl whom I did not even know as a temporary measure to enable me to stay in America as a permanent resident. And so it was. Through a friend of my uncle, a young woman was found in Liberty, Indiana who agreed to marry me for $250. We all went to the Justice of the Peace where we were officially married. That was the first and last time I ever saw that woman because all the legal paperwork for my immigration status was handled by others. That, however, was not the end of my immigration adventure. I had to leave the country, go to Canada, go to the American Consulate and apply for re-entry to the United States as a permanent resident. My uncle decided to drive with me to Windsor, Canada where we stayed for three days and then went to Montreal to visit with my cousin Georgia and her family. After Montreal, we drove to New York City and visited with my cousins Peter, Katherine and Mary. We stayed in New York for three days and then drove back to Middletown after stopping to see relatives and friends of my uncle along the way.

Getting married as I did was totally against my principles, my conscience, and my ethical standards, and it weighed heavily on me for several years thereafter. Except for my uncle, my Thea Marigo, my friend George Kilavos in Valparaiso, and my family in Greece, no one else knew how I managed to stay in this country. I knew that it was wrong to get into a marriage of convenience, but I convinced myself that it was the only choice available to me.

You Are in the Army Now

After I returned to Valparaiso from Middletown, I contemplated my future. I started looking for a job in Valparaiso, but there was nothing available for me. Weighing all my options, I even went to Chicago and applied for a job at the Chicago Transit Authority but did not hear anything from them. At that time Valparaiso University was looking for people to paint the interior of some of the buildings before the start of the fall semester. I decided to take the job painting interiors of classrooms and dormitories. At the end of the summer of 1958, not being able to find another job and after a discussion with my aunt, I volunteered for the army since I knew that sooner or later I would be drafted. In August I received my notice to report to the draft board in Valparaiso, and on September 2, 1958 I boarded a bus with several other young men to go to the induction center in Chicago.

After a physical examination, we were sworn into the United States Army, and on the same day we were taken to a train that took us to a town close to Ft. Leonardwood, an army base in Missouri. During the whole process of that day, I actually felt very good and was proud to join the army. I always believed that every young man in America should have the opportunity to give at least two years of service to his country like they do in Greece. Besides, going to the army would give me an opportunity to test my abilities and courage. I really never had the opportunity to test myself for courage, and down deep I was hoping that I would be sent somewhere where I would be tested in combat conditions. Of course that did not happen because at that time we were not engaged in any conflicts.

It seemed that we were on the train forever, but I met some very nice guys my age and we played cards until we arrived at the army base in Missouri. As soon as we got to the base, they took us to the mess hall where we had our first army food. Some of the guys complained about the food, but I sort of liked it. We stayed in Ft. Leonardwood for a week where they administered a series of tests before some of us were shipped by bus to the army base in Ft. Hood, Texas and assigned to the 35th Artillery Co. of the 2nd Armored Division.

We arrived at Ft. Hood at 2:00 A.M., and after we were taken to the mess hall for more army food, we were led to our barracks which would be our home for the next eight weeks. There were two rows of double bunks with ten bunks on each side. The bedding for each bunk was rolled up on the top of the springs of each bed. When we got into the barracks, we found the floor almost covered with large crickets, thousands of them. The bedding was also covered with those creatures. The drill sergeant ordered everyone to sweep the floor and the bedding clean of the crickets and go to sleep immediately. The lights went out, and at 6:00 in the morning we were woken up by the sergeant who was also to be our drill instructor during our basic training. We were told that we had half an hour to get up, make our beds, go to the bathroom, take a shower, shave and get ready for reveille at the parade grounds outside the barracks. We all got a small dose of what our life would be during our basic training.

The next day we were lectured on what the army expected from us and our behavior around the company area. For the next ten weeks we had to carry our rifle with us everywhere we went within the company area. The uniform was to be worn properly and kept clean when worn in the area. We had to salute every commissioned officer and address him as "Sir." We had to run everywhere we went within the company area and do ten push-ups before going to the mess hall for any meal. If we failed to comply with these rules, we could be ordered by any member of the company cadre to hit the ground and do ten push-ups. If the push-ups were not done properly, they had to be repeated. I really did not have a difficult time with any of the above regimentation. When I went to the army, I weighed 177 pounds; after ten weeks of basic training, I weighed 143 pounds.

The word got around that Elvis Presley was also in the same company with us, but he had already completed most of his basic training. His platoon was in the next barracks, and all of us hoped to have a chance to meet him. Twice when some of us went to the Post Exchange (PX) to relax after a whole day in the field, Elvis stopped at our table and sat with us. Seeing that we did not have money for a beer, he ordered a couple pitchers of beer for us. He made such a good impression on all of us. There he was a famous singer and actor known the world over, and he was talking to us like a regular person. Elvis was liked by everyone in the entire company, and I will always remember him as a personable, friendly, and gentle guy.

I was informed that I could claim my parents in Greece as dependants if I had been providing them with any type of financial assistance before joining the army. The truth was that I always managed to save some money to send them when I worked in the summers and during the school year. I told that to the army and they told me that my parents were eligible for assistance if I wanted it. Naturally I said, "Yes." The army was to take 80% of my pay, match it, and send the money to my parents in Greece. Being declared as my dependants made them eligible to shop at the American Post Exchange (PX) in Athens where the GIs and their families were doing their shopping. Another benefit that my parents received was the ability to see American doctors and receive medical treatment with nominal cost to them.

I can honestly say that my time in the army helped me as a man and instilled patriotism in me which, unfortunately, some of today's young people do not have. I managed to get along with just about everyone in my platoon, with one exception. There was one fellow who was a little bigger than I was who was constantly making fun of me because of my accent. I ignored him most of the time until he called me a "greasy Greek." That made me angry. He was standing next to my bunk, and I got up and hit him really hard in the stomach with my fist. When he bent over, I hit him again on the back of his neck with my right knee and he fell on the floor. I helped him up and he never gave me any trouble after that. In fact we became friends. I could have gotten in trouble for what I did, but the incident was never reported to the platoon leader.

After a few weeks in the army, I noticed that it was painful to wear the top of my fatigues or uniform. It was even more painful to take a shower. I noticed that the right side of my chest was covered with little blisters, so I went to the medical dispensary in our battalion. The doctors sent me to the base hospital where I was diagnosed with "Herpes Zester" commonly known as shingles. I was kept in the hospital for ten days and then sent back to my unit. While in the hospital, I took off my high school class ring that had been given to me by my classmates and placed it on top of the sink while I washed my hands. I forgot to put my ring back on when I left the bathroom. When I realized that I was not wearing it, I went back to retrieve it, but unfortunately it was gone. Although I reported it to the nurse, there was nothing she could do. I had always worn that ring with pride because it had been given to me by my entire high school class, and it had great sentimental value to me. I was very sad to lose it.

At the end of my basic training, I was transferred to another unit and assigned to the administration office of a combat command. It was there that I met George Kacos who was also from Greece and had come to the United States after an invitation from an uncle who lived in Connecticut. He told me that his relationship with his uncle was not that great and that he had actually been happy to receive the notice from his draft board. George was a talented cook, and he was assigned to the headquarters company mess hall. The menu for all meals was the same everywhere there was an American army, and the recipes for each meal were also the same. George soon became the head cook of our company, and although he followed the army recipes, he managed to add that something extra that made the food taste better. It did not take too long before many officers from other units started coming to George's mess hall for their meals.

George and I became good friends. We even managed to pool our money and buy a 1946 Chevrolet that was barely running. We took it to the motor pool, and in the evenings, after being relieved from our jobs, we went to the motor pool where we took the car's engine apart piece by piece. With the help of some of the mechanics who were there, we threw away all the bad parts and replaced them with whatever we were able to find in the local junk yards. We had a hard time putting the engine together, but with some help we managed to get it right and mount it in the car. That car became our means of transportation to and from Dallas, Waco, and other cities around Fort Hood where we usually went for a weekend in town. We had very little money, but we made friends everywhere we went and always had a place to sleep.

George was discharged from the army a month before me. Because he did not think that our car would make it to Connecticut, he asked me to keep the car and pay him $150 when I could. And so I did. I kept the car, and when I was discharged from the army, I drove it to Valparaiso and later to Middletown. My uncle had been given a 1954 Buick by the court after someone had broken into his house and stolen money and other valuables. The burglar was caught, but the only thing he had was a car. He was not able to give back what he had stolen, so the judge gave my uncle the only thing that the burglar had. I paid my uncle $300 for the car, and I sold the car that brought me from Texas for $250. I was discharged from active duty, but I was not discharged from the army. I had to serve in the active Army Reserves for two years and then another two years in the inactive Reserves.

Life after the Army

My active army career was over, and I now had to think about what to do with the rest of my life. After my discharge from the army, I drove to Valparaiso with the intention of finding a job, making a living there, and continuing to help and support my aunt who was getting older and needed to have someone close to her. I made my resume and contacted some of the local companies for potential employment opportunities. I also applied for work at some of the steel companies in Gary, Indiana. After three months of fruitless effort to secure employment, I discussed my situation with my aunt and I made the decision to go back to Middletown and seek employment there. I promised my aunt that I would never forget her for everything that she had done for me and that I would come back every other week to spend the weekend with her, which I did faithfully. I had always kept in touch with my friends in Middletown, and I knew that I would at least be able to establish a good social life there and potentially meet a girl that I would eventually marry.

In 1955 my uncle encouraged me to become a member of the American Hellenic Educational Progressive Association (AHEPA). The first Saturday of each May, the Middletown Chapter sponsored a dance called the May Festival and Queen Coronation which was attended by several hundred people not only from Middletown, but also from several cities in the area such as Cincinnati, Dayton, Springfield and others. Each chapter of AHEPA from these cities submitted the name of a single, young lady to represent its chapter in the pageant where one of those young ladies would be chosen as the May Festival Queen. The judges were usually radio and TV personalities or even a movie star if he or she happened to be in the area. When the girls did not bring an escort from their hometown to walk with them as part of the pageant, the younger and single members of the Middletown Chapter were asked to fill the role of the escort. I was asked to escort one of the candidates twice, which gave me the opportunity to meet them and have a dancing partner at least for part of the evening. In May of 1962 my sister Potoula was expected to be in Middletown, so my Uncle George and I sponsored her as a candidate for queen at the May Festival. She won and was crowned as the queen by a Hollywood movie star who happened to be in the area.

Soon after I returned to Middletown, AHEPA sponsored a luncheon in the basement of the church. The luncheon was attended by several AHEPA members from Dayton and Cincinnati. The younger members were assigned the job of serving lunch to everyone present. There I met a gentleman from Dayton, Mr. Louis Preonas, who owned a plant where they made pies and cakes that were sold to restaurants and other places in Dayton, Columbus, Louisville and Indianapolis. He introduced himself and asked me questions about where I was from and where I worked. When I told him that I did not have a job, he gave me his card and asked me to come to Dayton and see him at his office which I did the following Monday.

He gave me a job in accounting, and that was my first job following my army tour. I continued to live with my uncle in Middletown and commuted to and from work with the Buick that I had bought from him after the burglary of his house. A year later, I was sent to Indianapolis to perform basically the same type of work, and in between times I was sent to Hammond and Ft. Wayne, Indiana for various work assignments. Everywhere I was sent, I had to rent a room in a boarding house because in most cases I was not given a per diem allowance and my salary did not allow me to live in anything better.

While I was in Indianapolis, my army friend George Kacos came to visit me. He told me that he had had an argument with his uncle who had invited him to America, and he had decided to leave Connecticut and come to Ohio, find a job and live there. The following weekend, we drove to Harrison, Ohio where my second cousin John Lenardos, who had lived with my family during the war, was a partner at a restaurant. It so happened that he was looking for someone to run the kitchen and do the cooking in the night shift. George was hired immediately.

Starting My Life's Work

After I started working in Dayton, I decided to enroll in Xavier University's MBA Program in the evenings. Mike Revelos also was attending the same program at Xavier, and we commuted to and from our evening classes together. While attending Xavier, I was notified that

I had to report one night a week to an Army Reserve unit in Hamilton, Ohio. That made it difficult for me to work in Dayton, attend classes at night in Cincinnati, and attend Army Reserve duty one night a week in Hamilton. I did that for a few months, but after a while I decided that I was spreading myself too thin and decided to quit the MBA Program and return to the program later. I only lacked four courses in order to receive my MBA. A year later I was released from the active Army Reserves, and I decided to move from Middletown to Dayton. A man my age who also worked for the Blue Bird Baking Company and I found an apartment where we could share the rent.

The owner of the apartment was an older lady, and every Friday and Saturday night she ran a poker game in the basement of her house. We soon became aware of this because on those nights we would see several men going into the house, but they did not come out. They would go to the basement, which was soundproof, where the landlady kept a round table covered with a green felt cloth with holes around it to hold the beer glasses. Naturally, she took her share of any pot, no matter who was the winner. On poker nights, she would prepare sandwiches, cheese trays, sometimes cooked food and give us money to go buy beer for the poker players. If we had no plans for the weekend, she would invite us to her place to have dinner with her and share the food that she was serving the poker players.

A few times when we happened to be there, the police raided her house because gambling was illegal. When the police came and knocked on the door, Pauline would take her time answering and with a button in her kitchen she would notify the gamblers that the police were coming down. Next to the gambling room she had built another room that was well-ventilated and separated from the other room with a wall so carefully constructed that it was impossible to notice its existence. When the signal was given from upstairs, everything was picked up and everyone moved to the hidden room without leaving a trace that gambling was taking place. Once in a while, my friend and I would go in the basement and watch the poker game, but we never played because those guys were playing for high stakes which we could not afford.

Returning to America 1952

With Thea Marigo
High School Graduation

With Uncle George
and George Tsuturas

Jim Kilavos, George Kilavos, Bob Platt, Kondilo's brother,
George Pulos and me in Valparaiso 1955

College Graduation
1958

Army Days 1959
2nd Armored Division

LIVING THE AMERICAN DREAM

Meeting My Future

In October 1961, my cousin John Lenardos announced his engagement to a young lady from Springfield, Ohio. Her parents had an engagement party for the couple in their home in Springfield. My uncle and I and a few mutual friends from Middletown were invited to the party. There were several young women there, and the guys were all asking them to dance. I spotted one of them and got the courage to approach her and ask her to dance with me even though she looked much younger than me. I introduced myself and she also introduced herself as Diane Babalis. She was a sophomore attending Wittenberg University Although I guessed that she was about eight years younger than me, I sort of liked her, and we danced together repeatedly until the end of the party. We both went our separate ways, and although she was in and out of my mind for a while, I really did not think that she had any interest in me.

John asked me to be an usher at his wedding, along with George Kacos and some other friends. At the wedding rehearsal, much to my surprise, I saw that Diane was also in the wedding party and was paired up with my friend George Kacos. Later I found out that they had double-dated with John and Sandy a few times. I was to escort another young lady, but my eyes were set on Diane.

I had never met Diane's parents, and I thought I would have the opportunity during the reception to meet them. The wedding party was seated at a long table higher than the guests' tables. To my surprise, I found myself sitting between the girl I was escorting and Diane. I got the feeling that Diane did not want me to talk to her very much, perhaps because her escort was sitting on the other side of her. It so happened that Diane's parents were seated directly in front of us. When dinner was over and we stood to leave the dais, I leaned over the table and introduced myself to her father. I think he told me in Greek that he was glad to meet me, but I was not able to read his body language as being positive. He was probably wondering why some stranger was introducing himself.

The band started to play and we all started to dance with our partners. After a while, I asked George if it was okay to dance with his partner, and Diane and I danced one or two dances together. The call came out for all the single men to try to catch the bride's garter. The garter landed in front of my feet. I bent and picked it up and put it in my pocket. This was followed by the bride throwing her bouquet to all the eligible women. Diane caught the bouquet, and following tradition, the two of us danced together for one dance. However, it turned out that we continued dancing together until the end of the reception. I asked Diane if I could take her home, and she told me that her escort was supposed to take her. The three of us left the reception together, but when we got to our cars, I just took her by the arm and said I would take her home. George did not object because it was obvious that I had developed a very strong interest in Diane. I drove her home and parked in front of her house. We talked for a long time learning things about each other.

We corresponded a few times in the next couple of weeks. The GAPAs in Dayton always had a big Christmas Ball. Since Diane's married brothers lived in Dayton, I asked her if she would be going to the dance. We made plans to meet at the dance. Her brother John picked her up in Springfield and brought her to the dance. Soon after that, we had our first actual date.

I did not have much money to go out to dinner and then to a show, but on our first date we did go to the restaurant at the Holiday Inn. I was falling in love with Diane, and I wanted to tell her the secret that I had kept for a long time from most of the people that I knew. I had to come clean with her if our relationship was to be based on trust and honesty. And so at the end of our dinner, I told her that in order to stay in America, I was married to a woman from Indiana in a convenient but legal marriage that a friend of my uncle had arranged. I noticed a tear coming down her cheek and thought that our relationship was over before it really began. I told her that I had developed some very strong feelings for her, but I would understand if she did not want to see me again. She did not say whether she did or did not, but she did ask me for details about everything concerning my marriage of convenience. I answered all her questions honestly, but when I took her home, I did not know how she felt about me or the news which I had told her. Driving back to Middletown, I kept hoping that with everything I had told her after dinner, she would still want to see me. The following week I received a much anticipated letter from Diane in which she did not even mention anything about the topic of our discussion. I found this very encouraging, and from then on I went to Springfield almost every Saturday to see her and go to a movie together. When I moved out of my uncle's house in Middletown and moved to Dayton, it made it much easier for me to go to Springfield.

During our courtship, I tried to be on time for our dates, but somehow I always managed to be late which did not make Diane very happy. She was and is a very punctual person, and she could not understand how anyone could be over an hour late for anything. My tardiness also irritated her father. He used to say, "He seems like a nice boy, but he has no sense of time." After months of never being on time, I decided to do something. One week, without telling Diane, I showed up on Friday night instead of Saturday night. Needless to say, Diane was totally surprised when she came to answer the door with wet hair and wearing a housecoat. The only explanation that I gave for coming a whole day early was that I was making up for all the times that I had shown up late. Diane found this amusing and did not show any sign of being angry.

The Babalis Family

Diane's father was from the Greek province of Roumeli, which is located in the central-west part of Greece, and had come to America in the early 1900s. Her mother came to America in 1921 after leaving her home in Constantinople, present day Istanbul, when the Greek population in Turkey was being persecuted by the Turks. The two met in Springfield, Ohio and were married in 1922. They settled in the same town and had four children. Gus was the oldest, followed by Elizabeth, John and then by Diane who was twelve years younger than her youngest sibling. When I met Diane, both Gus and John were married with children and lived in Dayton, Ohio. Elizabeth was single and lived in Los Angeles. Diane was the only sibling living at home.

When I met Diane, she was a sophomore in college. It was obvious to me that Diane was very intelligent. Her professors were encouraging her to go to graduate school so that she could become a college professor of history or philosophy. I was willing to wait for her to graduate from college, but graduate school was out of the question. She finally decided to major in French and get a teaching degree so that she could teach upon graduation, and we planned to get married when she finished college in June 1964.

Diane's parents, Steve and Domina Babalis, were always very nice to me. Mr. Babalis always gave us a pass for one of the two movie theaters in Springfield. The theaters were owned by good family friends. Therefore, Diane and I got to see new movies by paying only ten cents each. Mrs. Babalis was a great cook, and she always invited me to have dinner with the family when I went there on Saturday nights. I was invited to join the family for holiday dinners, whether they were held at their home or at Gus's or John's home. I began to feel very comfortable around the whole family, and everyone treated me like a member of the family. The first time I went to Thanksgiving dinner at John's house I disappeared into one of the bedrooms after dinner and fell asleep for a whole hour. I woke up when someone opened the bedroom door to see if I was still there. I was a little embarrassed when I went to the family room and everyone was asking me if I was okay.

Living in Springfield

The Blue Bird Baking Company where I worked in Dayton was a family-owned company with very limited opportunity for me to advance any higher than my current position of accountant. I made up my mind to look for another job that would present me with more opportunities for advancement. A friend of mine who lived in Springfield asked me to go work for the finance company where he worked. I went there and applied for a job and was hired. I moved out of my apartment in Dayton and moved into the Springfield YMCA until I found a one-room apartment in Springfield.

After I moved to Springfield, I had a standing invitation for dinner at the Babalis house. I really did not want to become a burden to Diane's family by going there for dinner every night and expressed this to Diane and Mrs. Babalis, but they told me that they liked having me there.

My title in my new job was Collection Manager, which meant that I had to contact by phone or personal visits the customers who had not paid their monthly payments for the cars or furniture that they had purchased on credit through the company, which was based in Cincinnati, Ohio. I learned my job quickly and became very good and efficient at doing it. At times I had to deal with some very rough customers who did not want to give up their car, but at the same time they did not or could not make their payments. I quickly determined who were the bad customers and those who I thought with some help on my part would be able to pay their debts.

Although I received many threats, the entire time that I worked in that branch office I always found a way to avoid physical confrontations. When many of the people that I had helped saw me on the street, they would call me by my name when they greeted me. I had become quite known to the police and many of our customers in Springfield. I can honestly say that I did a very good job for the company, and its Springfield branch became the cleanest of all the Ohio branches as far as delinquency was concerned.

This did not go unnoticed at the Cincinnati company headquarters. A vice-president came to Springfield and asked me to go to the Columbus, Ohio branch of the company and clean up their delinquency problems. He told me that I was to work in the Columbus office with its manager, but I would be reporting directly to him. I told him that he was putting me into a difficult situation, but he told me that he thought that people were making "funny" loans and wanted me to be his eyes and ears in that branch and keep him advised on any irregularities that I found.

So I moved to Columbus and stayed in a hotel for two weeks until Cincinnati received my hotel bill and told me to find another, less expensive place to live. I moved to the YMCA that was two blocks away from the office and very convenient because they had a really nice and affordable restaurant where I was able to have my breakfast in the morning before going to the office. I stayed there for three months until I was transferred back to Springfield.

My job in Columbus was more difficult because of the distances and not knowing the city well. As it turned out, I found some "funny" loans that were made to people who did not exist with addresses in cemeteries or empty lots. I worked the rest of the delinquencies the same way as I did in Springfield. My findings were conveyed to my superior in Cincinnati.

After I had identified all the bad loans, my boss came from Cincinnati and fired the branch manager and the loan officer. He sent two people from Cincinnati to take over the branch, and at my request I returned to Springfield to my old job.

Working as a collection manager was one of the best experiences that any young guy like me could get. I learned a lot about people and what made them tick. At the same time, I learned a lot about public relations, how to avoid physical confrontations, and how to turn bad situations to my favor. My salary was just enough to sustain me, but that job helped me to become a better, more compassionate person and taught me how to get along with people from all walks of life.

One night after I had moved back to Springfield, I went to Middletown to visit my uncle and see some of my friends. I stopped to see Mike Revelos, and with a couple of other friends we went out for coffee and pie. At that time Mike was working at the Wright-Patterson Air Force Base in Dayton as a computer programmer. While he was talking about his job, I became fascinated with the description of his work. When I saw an ad in the Dayton newspaper about learning how to program computers, I paid $1,000 and enrolled in that class. The course was offered by a school called New York Technical Institute located in the center of Dayton. Three nights a week for two months I drove to Dayton after work to attend school. When I finished my programming class, I continued to work at my job, but I wanted to look for another job as a computer programmer.

In December 1963 I decided that it was time to ask Diane's parents for her hand in marriage. I told them that I loved their daughter and that I would wait until after her graduation in June to get married. They told me that they approved of me marrying Diane, and from then on I called them Mom and Pop, which they liked. I had already bought a ring, and I formally proposed to Diane at the same Holiday Inn restaurant where we had had our first dinner two years before. After we had been engaged for a while, Mr. and Mrs. Babalis offered to let me stay in the spare bedroom in their house. I gladly accepted that offer because I was able to spend more time with Diane and save money by not having to rent an apartment. I did not have much money, and part of what I had I spent to buy the rings for Diane.

I wanted my Thea Marigo to meet the girl I was going to marry, so we decided to take a weekend trip to Valparaiso over the Christmas holidays to visit my aunt who at that time was in the hospital with an advanced case of breast cancer. She was very happy to see me and meet Diane. We spent the night with Uncle Tony and Thea Alexandra and their children which gave Diane the opportunity to get to know my relatives.

In January, I had a call from Valparaiso telling me that my Thea Marigo had died. Although I knew that she had breast cancer, I was still hoping that she would be well enough to attend our wedding. Unfortunately, that did not happen. I was glad that Diane and I had gone to Valparaiso and that Thea Marigo had the opportunity to meet her. I went to the funeral and suddenly I felt as though I were a total stranger in my aunt's home. I truly loved that lady. She was sweet and kind and will always remain in my mind as my second mother. Although I no longer lived in Valparaiso, I thought of it as my home away from home as long as my aunt lived. Now that page of my life had to be turned and a new page started making a life with my own family which began with my engagement to my future wife Diane.

Getting Married

At the Dayton Christmas Dance that Diane and I attended after our engagement, we saw Mike Revelos whom I asked to be my best man at our wedding. My future brothers-in-law John and Gus were also there and they congratulated us on our engagement. Diane's family made arrangements to have a formal engagement party at the hall of the Springfield church on my future father-in-law's name day in January 1964. All of my friends and close relatives and most of the people in Springfield were invited. It was a great party.

My family in Greece was very happy when they received my letter announcing my engagement. I must say that my parents were always very supportive of me and did not try to influence my decisions. The summer before I got engaged, my Uncle George had gone to Greece and had tried to convince my parents to talk me out of marrying Diane. He thought that I could "do better" because her family was not wealthy. My parents told him that they would never tell me whom I should or should not marry. My sister Potoula, who had met Diane on one of her trips to America, told my parents about Diane and her family and put their minds at ease.

After the wedding date was set for June 21, 1964, my parents started to make plans to attend our wedding. Unfortunately, my father was not able to come due to health issues, but my mother did. I drove to Chicago to pick her up at the airport and brought her to Springfield. The Babalis family welcomed my mother and insisted that she stay in their home. My mother arrived the day before Mother's Day and was in town for Diane's bridal shower. At the end of May she also attended Diane's college graduation. She spent several weeks at the Babalis house before moving with me to the apartment where Diane and I would be living after the wedding.

My mother and Diane's mother were very different, but they got along well. Diane's mother was more like my dad. She was self-educated and constantly learning. My mother was more like Diane's father. They had the same sense of humor, and my mother felt very comfortable staying with them. I was especially happy that Diane and my mother got along well. In fact, they developed a wonderful relationship through the years and a genuine, loving bond which is rather unusual between daughters-in-law and mothers-in-law. Although Diane had some issues with my dad, she and my mom were very close.

On our wedding day, Mike Revelos, my mother and I went out for a late lunch and lost track of time. We returned to my apartment to get ready only half an hour before the ceremony. Diane was already at the church, dressed and waiting, and I was out to lunch! Diane and her parents were used to me being late for our dates, but I did not think that they would be as understanding about being late for the wedding. Fortunately, we arrived at the church on time. However, right as Diane was getting ready to come down the aisle, I realized that I had forgotten to bring the rings with me. Her brother John went out to the narthex and offered her the option of using his rings. She, of course, said, "No thanks. I'm not getting married with someone else's rings." John immediately raced across town to my apartment and brought the rings for the ceremony to continue. Fortunately, Springfield is a small town. It was the hottest day of the year, and the church was not air-conditioned. It had rained the day before; the temperature was over ninety degrees and it was very humid. I believe I must have been the happiest person there because I did not feel the heat as our guests did. I cannot imagine what they were thinking when after seeing Diane at the back of the church ready to come down the aisle, she was suddenly gone. The two priests just stood in front waiting.

I was really happy to see so many of my friends and relatives who had come from long distances to be with me on my happiest day. I was so happy to see my mother, who had come all the way from Greece to be at my wedding, and my Uncle George Manos, who escorted her during the ceremonies. There were also other friends and relatives who were very dear to me. They were the Katsicopoulos family, my cousins Mary Kara from New York, Georgia from Canada, the Kilavos family from Valparaiso and others. The only close relative that did not come was my mother's brother Uncle Tony and his family from Hammond, Indiana. My mother was very upset when she did not see him at the wedding because he was the only brother she had still living. We never found out why they did not come.

The wedding reception was held at the ballroom of the Shawnee Hotel located in the center of Springfield. It was a great party and everyone had a good time. After the reception my father-in-law invited everybody who was still at the hotel to come to the house for a buffet and drinks. About fifty to sixty guests came to the house where Diane's mom had prepared a wonderful buffet. After everyone ate, a record player was brought out in the backyard, and the guests danced to Greek music on the large driveway until 4:00 A.M. It was almost another wedding reception. Folding chairs had been set up around the driveway and it had started to rain a little. My father-in-law said to me, "Who is going to pick up all those chairs?" He was seventy-four years old and exhausted from such a long and emotional day. Since everyone else had gone home, I had to stack up all the chairs in the garage before we left for our honeymoon.

We drove to the Imperial House north of Dayton where I had made reservations. That motel was located very near the home of George and Becky Katsicopoulos. Diane thought it would be funny if we rang their doorbell at 4:30 in the morning and said we had come over for coffee. Then we remembered that they had two small children, and we didn't want to disturb them. We did not know that the children were staying with their grandparents that night. Forty-five years later, Diane and Becky still talk about what an unforgettable moment it would have been if we had rung their bell that morning.

The next day we got a late start heading for Florida, so we had to stop in a small town in Kentucky. We will never forget Corbin, Kentucky. The room was so small you had to climb over the bed to get to the bathroom, and the air-conditioning unit extended over one third of the bed. We could not wait for morning in order to leave that place and continue our trip south. I had heard that Gatlinburg, Tennessee was a good place to go to enjoy the mountainous terrain and southern hospitality. We drove to

Gatlinburg, found a nice motel with a swimming pool and stayed there for five days. We still remember the wonderful apple butter there. After Gatlinburg, we drove to Daytona Beach, Florida and stayed across the road from the beach.

After our honeymoon, we moved into an apartment that Diane's mom had given us in one of the apartment buildings she owned. During our honeymoon my mother had stayed with my uncle in Middletown, but when we got home, she moved in with us for about six weeks. All in all, my mom stayed in America for about three months. When the time came for my mother to return to Greece, Diane and I drove her to Chicago, stopping first in Hammond, Indiana to visit with her brother Tony for a few days.

My Computer Career Begins

After we were married, we stayed in Springfield for only two months because I was transferred to Cincinnati to work in the headquarters of the Midland-Guardian Company. The company had been advised of my interest in computer programming and that I had attended classes at my own expense. They wanted me to come to Cincinnati to set up their computer operation. The company had ordered a non-IBM computer and brought in a technical person to teach me and another longtime employee the new symbolic language which was new to me and totally unknown to the other employee. In those early days, computers were so large that they took up a whole room. Before our computer came, I was sent to Memphis, Tennessee to see a similar computer in operation and then to Indianapolis to test the practice programs that I had written. My computer career began. While I was a visionary in things that we could do with the computer, I was also adventurous which led me to risky undertakings that fortunately paid off during my career.

Up to that time, the company officers and managerial personnel were accustomed to receiving what was known as the "Daily Report" which showed the company's business activity for the previous day and year-to-date. I was asked to write a program that would produce this report by the computer. It sounds like a simple assignment, right? It took me more than a couple of days and nights of hard work to make it a reality. By that time, I had made up my mind that this was the work that

I wanted to do and I had to excel in it. After successfully completing the "Daily Report," I wanted to convert all loan records that were only available on machine-printed 8"x12" cards to computer magnetic tapes. At that time that was somewhat of a revolutionary idea that I had to sell to management that wanted to let the manual system run its course and only the new accounts be put into the computer. I did not agree with that approach and asked for the chance to present a different option.

I decided that this would make or break my career. I started to think like a systems analyst and not as a computer programmer, which was my job. The company had not yet hired a systems analyst, and I wanted to have the opportunity to be that person. I was working twelve to fourteen hours a day with no overtime pay, six days a week and several hours a week at home. I believed then and during my entire career that I should give 100% effort to any task which I was paid to do. While I knew that I was giving much more than 100%, I made up my mind that in order to excel and get ahead in life, I had to be more productive in my new profession and prove myself worthy of promotions.

In order to have my plan approved and have my proposal funded by the company, I spent a considerable amount of my time working on a presentation to management. I also knew that I needed help. I worked with the computer company's representatives for direction, and I joined the local chapter of the Systems and Procedures Association where I met many professionals who had been in situations similar to mine. Through lectures and personal contacts, I had enough information to put together my presentation.

The presentation was made in a large, plush conference room, which in itself was somewhat intimidating, and was attended by the corporate officers and top-line managers. I basically placed my job at risk by making such a proposal. Everyone listened and asked many questions, which was a good sign that they were not bored or disinterested. They complimented me on my presentation and told me that they would get back to me in a few days.

A week later I was asked to attend another meeting to answer new questions about the proposal. Again the meeting was productive and the body language of all present seemed favorable. A week later I was advised by the financial officer of the company to proceed with the implementation of my proposal and to start interviewing computer programmers. I was also advised that my title had been changed to that of a Systems Analyst and my salary was increased immediately. The increase did not even come close to paying me for the hours that I worked, but it was a welcomed gesture that they approved of what I was doing and my work effort. That is how my career as a systems analyst started. For the next three years I worked tirelessly to improve my knowledge of systems and programming.

Family Life

In order to do the job that I wanted to do, sacrifices had to be made by both Diane and me. Moving to a strange city two months after our wedding, Diane spent many weeks by herself in a two-bedroom, second-floor apartment without air-conditioning. The week that we moved to Cincinnati the temperature was over 100 degrees for days. Our apartment was an oven. The first day that I came home from work, there was no dinner. Diane said, "How can you possibly eat in this heat?" I had been in an air-conditioned office all day, and I was hungry. There were no microwave ovens in those days and no easy meals. Once Diane realized that heat or no heat I wanted to eat, she had dinner prepared. Most of the time, I would get home very late, and after dinner I had to get some sleep in order to be able to function the next day. Even though I was dead tired, sleeping in that sweltering heat was not easy. We did not even have a fan. It is difficult for anyone who knows Diane now to believe, but that first August, in that unbearable heat and humidity, Diane would sit up all night fanning me so that I could sleep. She slept in the early morning after I went to work when it was a little cooler.

I owe a lot to my wife because she never complained about my small salary or being alone during the long hours that I worked. Later on when I started working on the conversion of data to the computer system, she would come to the office on the bus and bring dinner for both of us so we could eat together and talk to each other while I worked. She would separate the programming sheets or if there was nothing to do, she would read old magazines in the ladies lounge until I was ready to go home. We would walk up to Fountain Square and catch the midnight bus home. My salary was just enough to pay for the rent on the apartment, the groceries, the gasoline, which at that time was very inexpensive, and to have a pizza once in the while. Since we didn't know we were moving to Cincinnati until July, it was too late for Diane to get a full-time teaching job. She did some substitute teaching at Woodward High School because it was within walking distance of our apartment. However, most of the time, she stayed home alone.

In addition to coming to the office with supper and helping me go to sleep on hot nights, Diane helped me with the documentation of the systems on which I was working. Because the systems were to be used by people not familiar with computer language, systems had to be well-documented and in a language that other people could understand. I wrote the documentation longhand, including the various means of system operation, and Diane, after asking me lots of questions so that she could understand everything herself, would rewrite it in very precise language that everyone could understand.

Whenever I did not have to work on the weekend, we would drive to Springfield on Saturday afternoon to spend the rest of the weekend with my in-laws and go the movies for ten cents. Before we were married, Diane had been the organist for the Greek Orthodox Church in Springfield for many years, and she and her family were held in high esteem by all the parishioners of that church. She felt very comfortable going to church there, and we made the decision to attend services at that church on Sundays and all major holy days. The weekend was also the time to see my brother-in-law John and his family and sometimes Diane's other brother Gus. Spending some time with Diane's family was very important not only to Diane, but to me as well because it gave me a feeling of family.

In the fall of 1965, Diane started teaching in the Norwood School District where she taught French for the next two years. We continued to live on my salary and saved all of her salary. She would endorse her paycheck and give it to me, and I would give her a small allowance. Although we did not spend her paycheck, it helped us financially because it took the pressure off of me to save money for the future. Saving money has always been very important to me. Having experienced the hardships of poverty when I was a child, I did everything I could to make sure that I would always be able to meet my family's needs. I saved as much of my salary as I could. We lived a very frugal life. It was more important for me to save for the future than to spend money on non-necessities in the present. Saving Diane's salary made me feel comfortable enough to go out to dinner sometimes. There was a Perkins Restaurant near our apartment which had daily dinner specials for about three dollars. It was a real treat for Diane when I came home for dinner at a decent hour and we could go there to eat. Her salary helped us save for the down payment on our first home and paid for a trip to Greece to see my family.

Diane's First Trip to Greece

Working twelve to fourteen hours every day and most of my weekends began to take its toll on my performance at work, and I was beginning to feel burned out. In the summer of 1966, I asked the company to allow me to take a one month vacation. After convincing them that my systems work for the conversion was complete, the documentation was in order and all the controls were set up for a successful implementation, my vacation was approved, and Diane and I flew to Greece to spend time with my family. That was the first vacation that Diane and I had since we were married.

When we arrived at the Athens airport, the entire family was there to greet us. Everyone's emotions were running high as we all embraced each other. That was the first time that my father and my brother-in-law Alexi met Diane, and they expressed their joy when they heard Diane speak Greek fluently.

After staying around my family's home for a couple of days and being visited by relatives and friends, Diane and I started to take the bus every morning to a beautiful beach named Vouliagmeni. Diane, who does not like water, was willing to wade in shallow areas. In the early afternoon, we would catch the bus and go home to have our lunch with my parents. Mom and Dad had an extra bedroom and bath for us. In the summertime the people in Greece take a siesta after lunch until about five o'clock in the late afternoon to avoid the summer heat which at times can be over 100 degrees. Diane could not get used to the siestas, and instead of sleeping, she spent the afternoons reading some old Readers Digests that she found in the basement.

Diane did not like daily life in Athens. She was used to American punctuality and could not understand that the bus would come "whenever," and if the driver did not want to stop, he didn't. She never could appreciate the attraction the ocean and the beach had for people. She went to the beach because I loved it and because there was nothing else to do. On her own, she would never set foot in the ocean. She could not believe that prices varied with the customers. Since she did not look Greek, salespeople did not know she understood Greek very well. She was appalled that they would charge tourists more than locals. The whole siesta routine was an incredible waste of time to her. She didn't understand how people went out to eat at 10:00 P.M., and the outdoor restaurants were not appealing with cats wandering around your legs. While most people are mesmerized by the blue of the ocean, she saw the rocks and brown dust and missed the green grass of home. The only bright spot for her was helping my mother take care of my sister's two-year-old son while she worked. I was happy to be home with my family, but it was a long, hot, boring summer for Diane.

We decided to go visit my family's village, Vrontama. We rented a car and drove through Sparta to Vrontama to visit my Uncle John, his wife and the many relatives that I had left behind. Our stay in Vrontama was very pleasant. As much as Diane did not like Athens, she liked the village very much. She loved the relatives there and they also loved her. In the evening, when the men would go to the taverna in the town square, the women would bring chairs outside and sit around in a circle telling stories and jokes. Not only being fluent in Greek, but also knowing Greek slang and old stories, Diane fit right in. I think my mom was happy to have her friends meet her "American" daughter-in-law. Sitting around laughing with those women was Diane's favorite part of the whole trip to Greece.

After we returned to Athens, we decided to go to the island of Rhodes with my sister, Potoula, and her husband, Alexi. We flew with Olympic Airways and in forty-five minutes we were there. We went to see the Acropolis of Rhodes located on the highest point of the island. The only way to go up to the Acropolis of Rhodes is by riding a donkey or walking up the very steep road leading to the top. Diane wanted no part of either of those options and waited in a little café at the bottom of the mountain. After we did a little shopping, we returned to Athens and prepared to go home to America.

When it was time for us to go home, we were faced with a strike by pilots and flight attendants of all the European and some American airlines. We were stuck in Athens and could not return home. I overstayed my vacation from work for more than two weeks until Potoula, who worked for Air France, found an Olympic flight going to Rome and from there an Alitalia flight to take us to Zurich, Switzerland from where it would be easier to find a flight for New York.

We said our goodbyes to everybody and left Athens on an extremely hot morning. When we arrived in Zurich, it was cold and we were dressed in summer clothes. TWA sent us to stay in a really beautiful hotel in the middle of the city at their expense. We got some of our warmer clothes out and went to see part of the city. At night we went out to eat at the nearest restaurant we could find. We stayed in Zurich for almost two days until we were finally notified by TWA to go to the airport to return to America. When we arrived in New York, we could not find a flight home until the next day. Since we were out of money, we spent the night sitting in the airport. The next day we finally arrived in Dayton, and after spending a day in Springfield with my in-laws, we returned to our home in Cincinnati.

Changing Jobs

When I returned to work, management had heard about the airline strikes in Europe, and they were fully aware that I was not going to return on the day my vacation ended. The system I had designed and left for implementation before I left, with the exception of the final test, was almost complete. Everything went the way I told management it would, which made me and management happy. The company informed me that I would not be paid for the two weeks that I was late coming back. I was somewhat disappointed at that news because my long hours of work for the last two years without any overtime pay were not given any consideration. However, my work ethic and hard work continued until I found a position with another company three years later.

I continued to work for Midland-Guardian until 1969. The company was basically family-owned, and the sons started to graduate from their colleges and came to work in positions with pay much higher than mine. It had become obvious to me that my chances for advancement were very limited, if not non-existent. I was contacted by a friend of mine in ASM who asked me to go work for The Drackett Company, which was a wholly-owned subsidiary of Bristol-Myers. He offered me a job as a Systems Project Manager with a higher salary plus benefits and a bonus at the end of each year. I gave my two weeks notice and left Midland-Guardian on very good terms with the company management and all my colleagues.

I Am a Father

On September 21, 1967 we became parents of a beautiful little girl whom we named Aspasia after my mother. We decided to call her Cia. When I called Greece to tell my parents about their grandchild, I was somewhat apologetic that she was not a boy. I am the last Karampas to carry on the family name, and I knew my father wanted a grandson to bear his name. My mother, however, scolded me for such nonsense and only wanted to know if the baby was healthy. She was very happy to have a granddaughter named after her. My best friend and koumbaro, Mike Revelos, and his wife, Tina, became her godparents.

Diane resigned her teaching position in order to devote her time to our baby Cia and eventually to other children that might follow. We both thought that it was more important for her to be at home with the children instead of having someone else look after them.

In 1969, we were expecting our second child, and our apartment was too small to accommodate two children. In addition, there was no place for Cia to play outside. After living in an apartment for five years, we made the decision to find a house with a yard where our children could play and meet other children in a neighborhood environment. After visiting several houses, we decided to buy a four-bedroom home in Anderson Township in the Summit Estates subdivision. We lived in that house for twenty-one years. It is where both of our daughters grew up, walked to elementary school, and then went to high school and college.

On November 4, 1969 we had our second beautiful little girl whom we named Domniki after my mother-in-law. We decided to call her Nickie. Nick and Lena Triantafilou had insisted on being the godparents before she was even born. At that time we were very good friends with them and continued to be good friends for several years until we somehow grew apart. Nickie never felt comfortable with her godparents and always thought that Cia got the better deal in godparents.

Although I worked long hours, when I was home, I really enjoyed playing with the girls. I loved to get down on the floor with them until one time Cia jumped on me and cracked some ribs. We would play in the leaves, build snowmen, and pick apples from our three apple trees. I always wanted to take them with me to run errands and could not understand why they never wanted to go to the hardware store. They did enjoy going to Fantasy Farm, a little playground near Hamilton that had rides and live animals. Of course, after King's Island was built, that became the prime destination. I loved being a father.

Owning My Own Home

It meant a great deal to me to have my own home. Once the war started when I was a very young child, I never had the stability of a permanent home. The houses I lived in were burned. We were constantly running from one place to another to hide from the enemy. After the war, we were too poor to have a home of our own. I loved being a homeowner. Although I worked very long hours, I still found time to work around the house.

When I took that first woodworking class in high school, I realized that I like building things. In my first house, I paneled the family room, made built-in bookcases and storage cabinets. Diane and I wallpapered several rooms which was much more challenging than I expected. She wanted the edges to match; I was more interested in just covering the walls. I wanted to finish the basement so that the girls would have some place to spread out their toys. I built a cedar closet, made storage shelves and lined two walls with bookcases. For several years the floor was covered with Barbie dolls and accessories. I was very focused on getting things done, sometimes at the expense of accuracy. Diane never hesitates to remind me of the two inch gap in the frame I built around the fireplace which I had to fill in with putty and cover with paint. In our second house, I only finished the basement. I had sold my saws and most of my tools when we moved. Diane had insisted.

My Parents' Trips to America

My mother's first trip to America was to attend our wedding. In 1972 my father made his first trip to America. He and my mother came to see their granddaughters and brought my sister's five-year-old son, Demetri, with them. My sister accompanied them in May to help them with Demetri and to get them through the airports. She stayed a few days and then in September Alexi came to accompany them on the way home.

I was very proud and happy to show my parents my life in America. We had sacrificed our time together as a family so that I could live the

American dream, and I was hoping that they would think that it had been worthwhile.

It was interesting to see America through my father's eyes. He finally understood what Diane was talking about on her trip to Greece when she said she missed the green grass. He was amazed at how green the landscape was. Single-dwelling houses with large lawns where children could play seemed like a luxury. In Athens most of the homes are apartment buildings or condos, and you have to go to a park to find any grass or a play area. My dad liked to explore. He would go for long walks through neighborhoods and business districts. He was impressed by the friendliness and honesty of the people. Not knowing the language or the money, he was surprised that store clerks would take just what they needed from his hand. He spent days looking through our World Book Encyclopedia page by page. Although he could not read English, he liked to look at the pictures and would ask about their significance.

My mother loved to look at all the housewares. Between the Germans and the Greek civil war she had lost everything several times, and when we fled to Athens, she did not even have a pot or a spoon for weeks. Ready-made clothes were also something new. In Greece, if she wanted a dress, she bought material and took it to a seamstress. Mom loved going shopping with Diane and finding dresses off the rack that fit her.

Both my parents loved spending time with the girls. My father complained that they could not communicate because the girls did not speak Greek. Of course it was Diane's fault because she spoke Greek fluently and should have taught them. My mother just loved looking at them, most of the time tearfully. They got to watch Cia get on the school bus for her first day in kindergarten. Nickie was almost three years old with long, very curly hair. They called her "katsaridaki" meaning "little curly."

On weekends I enjoyed taking my parents to visit friends and relatives. We usually went to Middletown to see Uncle George and the Revelos families. One day my dad and Uncle George went to visit Thea Sophia Revelos in the hospital. It was interesting to see three elderly people who grew up together in Vrontama laughing and joking like children many years later in Middletown, Ohio, USA. We took a trip to Springfield to visit my in-laws and attended the Greek Church picnic where my parents saw friends and relatives from Greece.

I took my parents and Demetri to Valparaiso. It was important to me to show them where I lived when I came from Greece and where I went to school. We visited with the Kilavos family, saw where Thea Marigo used to live, and then went to Uncle Tony's house in Hammond. We went to Chicago to a reunion picnic for people from Vrontama. My parents were overjoyed to see old friends and relatives. While in Chicago I also took them to the top of the Sears Tower. It was quite an experience for them. My parents' visit lasted almost four months. I was very happy to have this time with them. Since I left home at sixteen, every moment with them was precious. My mom made another trip here in 1974 when my Uncle George was dying and again in 1980 with my dad.

Visiting Greece with the Family

In the summer of 1978 my daughter Cia was ten years old and Nickie was eight. I wanted to take my daughters to Greece to see their grandparents and many other relatives whom they had not met. I managed to get four weeks vacation from Drackett, and in July we flew to New York and from there to Athens where my parents and Alexi were waiting at the airport. We were all happy to see each other, and we went to stay with my parents who lived in one of the apartments they owned in the area called Neos Cosmos. Alexi and my sister, Potoula, had moved to their new home in the suburb of Philothei which is considered one of the upscale areas in Athens.

A few days after we arrived, my cousin George Tsuturas and his daughter Lela arrived for their vacation and stayed with us for a week before they went to George's hometown, Zoupaina. George, the girls and I took a one-day cruise to three different islands, and the girls enjoyed being on the boat and visiting the three islands. Diane stayed home with my parents. We also went to see the Parthenon and other tourist sights in Athens.

In order to go to my hometown, Vrontama, I rented a small, four-door car that I drove all the way to the village. You have to imagine that there were six of us in that small car on curving mountain roads for five hours. To say that the trip was somewhat uncomfortable would be an understatement. Diane, my mother and the girls sat in the back and my father sat in the front with me. The car was not air-conditioned, and Nickie had to sit on Diane's lap the whole way. After a few hours we stopped at a roadside stand to eat and stretch our legs. The girls were shocked by the hole-in-the-ground restroom outside.

When we arrived in Vrontama, we were welcomed by my Uncle John, his wife, and several other distant aunts, uncles and cousins. The village had become Diane's favorite place in Greece to visit because she remembered the people she had met on our previous trip in 1966. She enjoyed the simplicity of the life in the village and the company she had with the neighborhood women in the evenings. My parents had built a small, two-bedroom house with indoor plumbing next to my grandfather's house where Uncle John lived, so we had a relatively nice place to stay.

I took my father, Uncle John and the girls on a few side trips around the area. It was important to me to show them the aloni where I used to play as a young boy. The biggest thrill for the girls, however, was riding my Uncle John's donkey and mule. My mother was very happy to have all of us there, and she made Greek pastries called "diples" for us and everyone who came to visit. The only negative part of our visit was the unbearable summer heat.

We decided to leave Vrontama and to go to Kosma, the village where I was born. The road going to Kosma was a twisting, narrow, one-lane, unpaved road that was quite challenging, especially when meeting another vehicle coming the opposite way. The trip took less than an hour, but when we arrived high in the mountain in Kosma, the temperature was much cooler than in Vrontama. The girls and Diane were very cold. My mother's sister lived in the house where I was born and took the girls to the second-floor bedroom and covered them with blankets.

Kosma is located at the top of Mt. Parnonas and our house is located on one of its highest points. My daughter Cia, looking down from the balcony, kept saying that we were so high that we were looking down on the mountains. The house had been burned down, along with all the other houses in the village, in January 1944 by the Germans. At the end of the war, we tried to at least put a roof on the house so that we would have a place to go in the summertime to avoid the heat of Vrontama. We had made some other minor improvements while I was still in Greece.

Our intention was to stay in Kosma for four days, but we only stayed for two. Diane felt very unsafe walking along the edge of a mountain, and the girls did not like the outhouse, especially in the middle of the night. The house had an unfinished ceiling, so little bits of dust, etc. kept falling on us. Of course, there was no electricity, no running water, or even a refrigerator. It was just too primitive for Diane and the girls. We spent two days and two nights in Kosma.

One morning I got up at 5:00 A.M. to capture the sunrise on film as the sun was coming up from the ocean beyond the mountains. The view was so beautiful that I used a whole roll of film. I had awakened the girls and Diane to watch this beautiful scene, but after one look, they said, "It's just the sun," and went back to bed.

I decided to return to Athens by a different route, through Leonidion. The road down the eastern side of Mt. Parnonas is very steep and narrow with no guardrails. We stopped at the monastery of Elona on the way down. It is cut into the side of the mountain. That is not a place for people with a fear of heights. Diane hated it not only because it was clinging to the side of a mountain, but also because she thought the monastery was more like a marketplace than a spiritual retreat. From Leonidion we took the scenic road by the ocean, also with no guardrails, and drove to the city of Argos then through Corinth back to Athens. Diane swore that she would never go back there again. After a few days in Athens, visiting with my parents, my sister and her family, and the Simonetos family with whom we later became good friends, the time had come for us to return to our home in Cincinnati.

My Girls

Both my daughters were good-natured and always well-behaved. They were good children who grew up to be good adults. They never caused any trouble or made us worry. We could not have asked for better children.

When Cia was a baby, we spoke to her only in Greek. She did not learn any English until we moved into our house when she was almost two. Once she started playing with other children in the neighborhood, she wanted to talk like them. By the time Nickie was born, we were speaking mostly English at home. Although both the girls can understand Greek and even speak a little, Cia still is a little better at it than Nickie. When they were in college, they participated in the College Year in Athens Program which required them to take a course in Greek. They spent four months studying in Athens. That reinforced what they already knew.

From the time they were little through high school we always celebrated both of the girls' birthdays by inviting their godparents for dinner, ice cream and cake. Those were really nice occasions because it gave the opportunity for our girls to bond with their godparents and their children. Cia's godparents, Mike and Tina, had three children about the same age as our girls. We were always invited to their children's birthdays in Middletown, which gave us the opportunity to see some of the Revelos family. Our girls enjoyed playing with Mike's children as well as Chris's and Lula's. Those were really great times that were so enjoyable for all of us.

Since George Manos lived alone and had cancer, we started going to Middletown to visit him on weekends. When he died, we continued going to church in Middletown every Sunday and visiting with Mike and Tina. Our families grew up together and are still very close. Our girls and Mike's children think of each other more as cousins than just friends, and Mike, Tina, Diane and I are like brothers and sisters.

Although both the girls were very good students, they had different talents. Cia was a free spirit and excelled in creative writing for which she won an award in high school. Nickie was more disciplined and excelled in advanced math classes. She was the editor of Anderson's yearbook her junior and senior year and named Outstanding Junior and Outstanding Senior. Both girls sang in the chorus, and Diane and I loved going to concerts.

Before we knew it, Cia and Nickie graduated from Anderson High School. They both chose to go to DePauw University in Greencastle, Indiana where they both pledged Kappa Alpha Theta. Cia majored in Psychology and Nickie majored in English and participated in an honors business program. Both girls were very good students and graduated in four years. Nickie was awarded membership in Phi Beta Kappa in recognition of her scholastic achievements.

At the beginning of her junior year, Cia was diagnosed with Guillian-Barré Syndrome. It is an autoimmune disease that usually follows the flu and causes paralysis. Her neurologist said that he had never seen the disease progress in the way it affected her. It somehow avoided her lungs which was almost a miracle. We were very grateful for all the prayers for her both here and in Greece. While in the hospital, Cia was visited by many of her friends from DePauw who drove three hours each way to see her. Diane stayed with her in the hospital day and night. When Cia was able to sit in a wheelchair, we brought her home.

Cia is a very determined person, and she wanted to return to DePauw and plan for her College Year in Athens (Greece) trip the following semester. She never doubted that she would do that. After several weeks of physical therapy, Diane took her back to school, and they allowed her to stay with a limited schedule. She still needed a cane, but she continued to improve rapidly. I truly admired Cia for her courage and her determination not to let her illness interfere with her overall plans. Through the grace of God and her hard work, Cia recovered fully and went to Greece for that spring semester.

Three years later, Nickie also went to Greece on the College Year in Athens Program, and I was very happy to have both of my daughters spend time in the land and culture in which I grew up. While there, they both had the opportunity to visit with their grandfather, aunt, uncle and cousins.

Upon graduation from DePauw, both the girls found jobs in Cincinnati. Cia worked at a Children's Psychiatric Facility and later as a social worker in Cincinnati while she attended Xavier University to receive her MA in Clinical Psychology. Nickie got a very good job at Fidelity Investments and was advancing rapidly. I can never fully express my pride in both my daughters.

Professional Activities

During my tenure of employment at The Midland Company and later The Drackett Company, I became a member of the Systems and Procedures Association, which was renamed Association for Systems Management (ASM). This organization benefited my knowledge of the systems profession through my association with members who had many years of experience in the field of systems analysis. I learned a lot from their experience, and I later became a systems professional respected not only by members of ASM, but by colleagues from non-member companies in the Cincinnati area. Eventually I developed my own system of steps to be followed when developing a new system. I applied this system personally in developing new systems while at Midland and later at Drackett. The word got around in the Cincinnati systems community and ASM chapters in cities in Ohio and Indiana. I was invited to be the guest speaker in Columbus, Mansfield and Toledo in Ohio, and in Indianapolis, Richmond and Columbus in Indiana. I enjoyed visiting those ASM Chapters because it presented me with the opportunity to meet other professionals and learn from them.

My association with ASM continued until my retirement. I served the Association well as secretary, vice-president and president of the Cincinnati Chapter and president of the Division Council. On the national level, I was elected vice-chairman and then chairman of the Eastern Region of ASM and was awarded the Distinguished Service Award (CSP). I also served four years on the Ohio Governor's Advisory Board for Computer Science Education in public schools.

After I started working for Drackett, I was contacted by Southern Ohio College to teach a class on Principles of Computer Programming at their night school. The salary was not that great, but I continued to teach that course for almost a year because I needed the money for my growing family. After a year, I was contacted by Cincinnati State College, a junior college and University of Cincinnati affiliate, to teach COBOL (Common Business Oriented Language). The pay was better than what I earned at Southern Ohio, so I accepted to teach an evening class for a year. At the end of each quarter the students were instructed to evaluate their instructors on their performance, and for each quarter my students gave me the highest possible evaluation. Because of my effectiveness as an instructor, at the end of the year, they offered me a 20% increase in pay to stay for another year.

About that time, the chairman of the Systems Analysis Department of Miami University (Ohio), with whom I had become good friends, asked me to teach a class in Introduction to Systems Analysis at the Hamilton, Ohio campus of the university with twice the pay offered by Cincinnati State. Naturally, I accepted his offer mostly because of the prestige associated with teaching at a well-known university. I taught there for two semesters with excellent evaluations from my students. After one year, I was asked to stay for another year, but due to my regular work's increasing demands and family commitments, I did not accept the university's offer.

I am very appreciative to both of my employers for sponsoring me by paying all my expenses for meetings, travel and other activities associated with ASM. I learned a lot from that association which made me a true systems professional, and the knowledge I gained I put to use to benefit my company.

George Karampas

My Job at Drackett

Soon after we moved into our home, I started to work for The Drackett Company, whose main offices were located on Spring Grove Avenue in Cincinnati. As I said previously, my job title was that of a Systems Project Manager, with the responsibilities of maintaining and implementing new systems for accounting, marketing, including market research, and sales systems. All systems up to that time were developed using symbolic computer language for programming which was becoming obsolete in favor of a relatively new language called COBOL which was more user friendly. I convinced my boss that we should look ahead and start the training of all systems and programming personnel in the new computer language and use it in developing all new systems.

At that time, the company had a large number of systems and programs that operated using the old symbolic language. These needed to be converted to the new language in order to provide maintenance and revisions to meet management's needs. The conversion was successful and everyone was quite happy with the results and my performance as the leader of that operation. The Information Systems Department was functioning well in maintaining old systems and developing new ones, which made everyone happy.

After a few years, the online information systems had started to attract the focus of corporate executives. This type of systems could provide them immediate access to business information they needed to make better and timely business decisions. The Director of Information Services asked me to spearhead the development of a database called IMS (Information Management System), the first of its kind in the company. This required another conversion of all the data to another way for the computer to look at, understand, and provide real-time information to those who needed it. The conversion was very successful and it even attracted the attention of the Bristol-Myers Company in New York, which complimented our department for having state-of-the-art systems.

All of the above came with long, tedious hours of hard work. Several times I worked as many as thirty-five straight hours and several weekends. Even when I went home, I would receive telephone calls from Computer Operations asking me for specific directions on operating the computer programs. Several times in the mid-seventies I felt that for better results I had to drive through several inches of snow to go to the office and solve problems. I took pride in my work, and the success of the systems for which I was responsible was my goal.

The Bristol-Myers Director of Information Services was advised of my good work, and one time he came to Cincinnati and asked me to go work in New York in his department. After discussing the offer with Diane, I decided not to accept because we did not want to raise our children in a big city. New York continued their interest in me and on three different occasions, after clearing it with my superior at Drackett, they asked me to accompany their internal auditors and perform audits with them, which I was happy to do.

In 1976, I was asked by the Director of Internal Audit of Bristol-Myers to help with the audit of Bristol-Myers Hellas in Athens, Greece. Travel arrangements were made for me in New York for first class accommodations, and I joined two other Bristol-Myers auditors whom I had never met before in Athens. The audit lasted four weeks, and I developed a very good work relationship with my colleagues and the people in the company we audited.

During the week we all stayed at the Athens Hilton which was the best hotel in Athens, but on the weekends, I went to stay with my parents at their home in Athens. I cannot forget any part of my stay with my parents during the audit period. It was so wonderful to be able to see the joy in my parents' faces seeing me sitting with them around the lunch and dinner table, asking questions about my family in Cincinnati, and telling me news about relatives and friends that I had not seen for a long time.

One weekend my parents asked me to invite my New York colleagues for dinner. My mother went all out to make the best dinner possible which impressed the two auditors very much. On a different weekend my father was invited to join the three of us on a one-day boat excursion to three islands. He was very happy to join us and we all had a great time.

The final week of the audit, we were visited by the Director of Bristol-Myers Internal Audit who came with his family for a short vacation and also to review the work that we had done. Through my sister Potoula, he found good hotel accommodations. At that time there were few available because of a large international convention that was being held in Athens. Potoula and Alexi invited him and his family to dinner, and they were very impressed with the food and the hospitality.

At the review, he was really impressed with my work. In fact, after we all returned to America, he sent me a letter of thanks and invited me to go to New York and work for him as an auditor. After discussing the offer with Diane, I again made the decision not to accept because we wanted our daughters to grow up in a smaller city. In 1986 and again in 1989, I was asked to perform audits in Puerto Rico for five weeks and in Canada for two weeks. In both cases my work effort and performance received high grades.

In the mid-eighties I became heavily involved with manufacturing and helped develop computer monitoring systems for all the production lines in our biggest plant in Urbana, Ohio. This also led to helping a consulting company with the development of a system that automated a new warehouse adjacent to the plant. That was one of my favorite systems because the warehousing of production and shipments out of the warehouse were so automated that almost all functions could perform automatically without manual intervention.

When I completed the work in Urbana, I was promoted to the position of Director of Internal Audit for Drackett. That job, however, only lasted for three years because our parent company, Bristol-Myers, decided to sell Drackett. Bristol-Myers wanted to concentrate more on pharmaceutical products, and Drackett's business in consumer products did not fit their long-range plans. And so Drackett was sold to the S.C. Johnson Wax Co. in Racine, Wisconsin, and 90% of Drackett employees found themselves out of work. I had managed to put money aside in my 401k plan sponsored by the company and financially I was in a fairly good position. I was fifty-eight years old, and those who were fifty-five or older were able to retire. That was the end of my corporate and my systems career.

Entrepreneur

Drackett, at that time, had office space in two buildings in Cincinnati: one on Spring Grove Avenue and two floors of the Atrium One Building in the center of the city. The lease for the two floors had another three years before it was up for renewal, and the company that had bought Drackett had to get out within three months in order to have it sub-leased to another company. All the furniture on the two floors was relatively new, and having worked in the financial area, I knew their cost. I approached the new owner representative and asked him what they were planning to do with all that office furniture. I was told that their plan was to hold an auction and sell all the furniture to the highest bidder. I knew that they did not have the time or the personnel to organize such an auction. I told them that there was no need to have an auction because I was willing to buy all the furniture on both floors. I offered an amount that I thought was very low, and I expected them to negotiate for a higher bid. They did not! They accepted my check and told me that the furniture on both floors was mine. I then asked my longtime friend Jim Demetrion to join me in this venture and receive 40% of the profit. And so it was.

We moved all the furniture into a warehouse in the north part of Cincinnati, advertised in all the papers, installed a liquidation sign in front of the warehouse and in three months we sold everything. This left Jim and me with a very good profit. I loved being my own boss and everything involved in this experience. It was a great venture and I looked for other similar opportunities, but I was not able to find anything that interested me.

George Manos' Death

My Uncle George Manos started to experience prostate cancer problems as early as 1962, and once every year he would visit a good oncologist at the Mayo Clinic in Rochester, Minnesota. Although the doctor had told him that he only had a maximum of two years to live, with proper treatments during the follow-up visits, he defied the odds and lived a relatively active life for eleven years until the end of 1973.

At the beginning of 1974, his health really deteriorated. I accompanied him to the clinic because he was in a lot of pain and was not even able to walk by himself. His doctor performed an operation and removed one of his kidneys. I stayed there for about ten days, and then my brother-in-law Alexi came all the way from Greece to stay with him for support. I had to return to my job.

Uncle George was released from the hospital after another week, and Alexi brought him back, by plane, to his home in Middletown. My mother had come from Greece to take care of Uncle George while he was at home. After Alexi returned to Greece, I drove to Middletown every day after work to help my mother with anything that I could. Thea Efthimia Revelos also stayed with my mother so that she would have someone with her to help all the time. Uncle George kept getting worse and was in and out of the hospital on a weekly basis. He died on May 21, 1974. My mother stayed with me until his Forty Days Memorial, as is customary in our church, and then returned to Greece.

The only major asset that Uncle George had was his house which was free of any mortgage and was included in a trust of which he had left me as the trustee. My cousin George Tsuturas was appointed as the administrator of his will. I had to sell the house, distribute some of the funds to people he had identified in the trust and divide the rest of the proceeds equally among my cousin Mary Kara, George Tsuturas and myself.

Karets

Uncle George had missed some very good opportunities in real estate when he was much younger, and he always regretted that he did not take advantage of those opportunities. Personally, I thought that the best investment for the money I received was in real estate. I did not want to regret it later that I did not learn from my uncle's mistakes.

I contacted a real estate agent and told him of my interest. This was the time that the Ford Motor Company was building a new transmission plant close to Batavia, Ohio, a small city about twenty miles east of Cincinnati. The agent called me and told me about thirty-two acres of land with a house that was available. I talked to George Tsuturas and Mike Revelos, and we decided to purchase it with all of us having equal shares. Using the first two letters of each of our last names, we established a partnership named "Karets." Two years later, believing that the demand for land would increase because of the Ford Plant, we bought another forty-four acres of land. Unfortunately, we were not able to do anything with the two properties due to high interest rates that followed and the introduction of much higher taxes by a new governor. The supply of available properties overwhelmed the demand. We did not want to sell the properties, thinking that things would get better and then we could sell them. We held the properties for a long time, and in the year 2001 we sold five acres to a friend of mine who built a mini storage warehouse and later another eight acres to a moving and storage company.

Mike and I, knowing that we were all getting older with children and grandchildren, thought of creating a limited liability corporation (LLC) to protect our personal assets from lawsuits in case of accidents on the property. Each of the partners' ownership would be identified with equal shares. We discussed this with my cousin George, and all of us agreed that we should proceed with the preparation of the necessary legal document. I contacted an attorney who prepared the legal document and presented it to all the partners, including the wives, to sign it. Everyone signed the document except for George's wife, who refused to have anything to do with it. George followed suit and recalled his signature from the document giving as a reason that Mike and I were not to be trusted.

We offered several suggestions for changes, but unfortunately, nothing was acceptable to George and his wife. This created a problem between my cousin George and me and Mike. We saw that it was impossible to have a good business relationship with George and his wife, so Mike and I decided to buy George's and his wife's shares of the partnership for a price much higher than its established value. In August of 2001 we all signed the necessary documents, paid George and his wife the agreed price, and then Mike and I and our wives became the sole owners of Karets, Ltd.

Although this measure was the best thing for all of us, it destroyed my relationship with my cousin to the extent that he did not even want to talk to me, in spite of my many efforts to approach him and try to reason with him. This is a burden that I have carried in my heart for years because it affected not only the two of us, but our families as well.

George was diagnosed with cancer at the beginning of 2007. When I heard, I went to see him in the hospital, and when he came home, I called him often and asked if there was anything that I could do to help him or his family. Unfortunately, cancer went to his liver and in January 2008 he passed away. This hit me hard in my heart because it did not give us a second chance to be as we were before when we both were in good health. He was a good man. Unfortunately he married a person who did not share his culture, customs, religion and Greek relationships which were so dear to his heart. I truly loved my cousin and I hope and pray that God will bless his soul.

Mike and I eventually sold the house on the first property for a good price. The rest of the land, about fifty-eight acres, is currently for sale if a buyer wants to pay what it is worth. It is free and clear of any debt which makes it easier for us to hold on to it until we get the right price or it is inherited by our children.

Bible Study and Poker

In the late 1970s Diane and other women from Middletown started a Bible study group. After a few months some of the women wanted their husbands to attend. At first, I was a little skeptical about attending. I thought that the men could play poker while the wives had Bible study in another room. But eventually I reluctantly went along with the other men. I thought that I knew enough about religion already since I had been an altar boy for many years and my mother had taught me to pray. I was surprised to find out that I actually knew very little.

The Bible study group included five to seven couples, all friends of ours for many years. We took turns meeting in each other's homes. Diane was always the designated leader because she knew more about the Bible than the rest of us. At that time Diane was working for a Catholic priest who lived in France, translating and editing several of his books and music from French into English to be used in the Catholic churches in America. He was a biblical scholar, professor of dogmatic theology, and a liturgist. In order to do her work, she had to use the Bible almost daily as a reference. The knowledge that Diane gained from her work became very beneficial for teaching us. I must admit that Diane gave me considerable knowledge about Christianity that I did not have before. I will always be grateful to her and the rest of the group for the religious knowledge I gained from those Bible studies that I attended. We met once a month for about fifteen years. We still see most of the members of our Bible study group socially and continue to be good friends.

When I transferred my AHEPA membership from Middletown to the Cincinnati Chapter, one of the first AHEPA members I met was Gus Skufis who took me under his wing and introduced me to members of the entire community. Gus and I became good friends and our friendship continued until his untimely death in 1989. Gus called six of his friends and asked us to start the Hellenic Poker Club which still exists to this day. Some of the original seven members have moved and some others have passed away. Whenever we lose a member, we ask another friend to join our group. We still play nickel/dime poker games once a month at the home of a member. We always have a great time at these games and enjoy good fellowship with each other.

The Simonetos Family

In the early eighties, my brother-in-law Alexi, who was a senior officer in the Greek navy, was sent to Washington, D.C. as the Greek Naval Attaché. He was stationed there for two years. Since my sister was coming to set up an apartment for him, their good friends the Simonetos family thought that it would be an ideal opportunity to visit America. I had met the family in Greece, so I invited them to stop by Cincinnati on their way to Washington. After they arrived in Cincinnati, we learned that Alexi's apartment would not be ready on time. This delay made it necessary for my sister and her two boys and Mally and Gaby and their two boys to stay with us for ten days. Four teenage boys, two teenage girls and five adults made a very lively household.

That visit was the beginning of a wonderful, close friendship with the Simonetos family. Diane and Mally bonded quickly and remain very close friends. We also became close with Mally's oldest son Andreas who has visited us many times over the years. He has stayed with us for months at a time while pursuing advanced dental studies here.

On my trips to Greece, Mally is my dentist. Due to poor, or should I say non-existent, dental care in my youth, I have needed extensive dental work, and she does outstanding work which impresses my dentist here. When I visit Greece, I look forward to staying with them at their beachfront home on the island of Spetses.

The Girls and I Go to Washington

When Alexi was in Washington, I thought it would be a good opportunity to take the girls to visit the nation's capital. Cia asked to bring along a girlfriend. Diane chose not to come. She was busy with a translating job at the time, and she thought work would be more fun than my so-called vacation. What was I thinking when I decided to drive ten hours in a car with three young teenage girls?

After we arrived at Alexi's apartment, he called Diane to ask what he should cook for dinner. She laughed and told him that was his problem. She knew what she was doing when she stayed home. The girls still remember Alexi trying to use ketchup as spaghetti sauce.

I wanted to go to museums, the Capital, the Lincoln Memorial and the White House. The girls wanted to go to the mall and the pool. It was very frustrating. The morning of our trip back home, I scratched my eye putting in my contacts. I stopped at a hospital in West Virginia where they put a patch on my eye. I had to drive ten hours through the mountains in the rain with one eye and the noise of three girls. I will never forget that trip.

My Parents Die

Diane called me at my office on June 18, 1982 and told me that our good friend Mally from Athens had called to tell her that my mother had passed away. I left work immediately and went home to make arrangements for my trip to Athens to be there for my mother's funeral. I called my father and sister and asked them to delay the funeral for two days so that I could be there. I managed to make my reservations, and the next morning I was on my way to Greece. I was quite emotional on the plane because although I had been away from the family for many years, I always felt close to my mother as if I had never left Greece. A movie kept playing in my head with all the good times we had from the time I was a little boy to the day I left for America.

The announcement of my mother's death was not a big surprise to Diane who always had a very special place in her heart for my mom. A few weeks before she died, I had called my mother, and both Diane and I spoke to her on the phone. For the first time ever, she said that she was not feeling well but never mentioned the reason. I told her that I planned to come and see her and Dad later that summer. After our call, Diane told me that I should go to see my mother as soon as possible because she would be dead by the time I planned on going. Diane somehow sensed something from our conversation with my mother that I did not. As it turned out, my mother died from a massive heart attack. On her last trip to America in 1980 my mom felt sick on the plane. We took her to a doctor and he said she was fine. After she went back to Greece, her doctor found heart problems, but I was never told about her condition.

My sister had made all the arrangements for the funeral which took place in Athens. For the first time in several years I saw many of my relatives and friends from Vrontama who came to pay their respects to my mother, who was very well-liked and loved by them. My mother wanted to be buried in Vrontama, but my sister wanted to keep her in Athens. It is the custom in Greece, because of limited permanent burial space, to bury bodies in temporary graves for three years until only the bones remain. There is no embalming. After three years, the bones are exhumed, washed in wine and placed in a small box for permanent burial. When it was time to put my mother in her final resting place, we made arrangements for a marble burial vault to be built in Vrontama, and we took her bones there, to the village she loved.

My father was totally devastated by my mother's death. Since he was so much older than her, he just assumed he would go first. Mom used to joke with Diane saying that she wanted to go first because he wasn't capable of boiling water. According to the customs of their generation and culture, she waited on him hand and foot. They had been married for forty-nine years and he was lost without her. My sister took him to live with her and her family.

I wish I had had the chance to tell them both together how thankful I was to have had them as parents and how much I loved them even from far away. I could stay in Greece for only two weeks because that was all the time I could have off from work. After my return, I had my mother's Forty Day Memorial in our church in Cincinnati, and my sister had the same memorial for my mother in Athens.

When my parents returned to Greece after their visit in 1980, they went to Vrontama immediately. My dad rode out to check on the olive trees and fell off the donkey, hitting his head on a rock. He did not tell anyone what had happened. I think he was embarrassed that he had fallen. A few weeks after they had returned to Athens, he started acting irrationally and getting lost. After many tests he was diagnosed with a subdural hematoma. Two holes were drilled in his skull to drain the blood. The pressure that had built up in his head had blocked blood flow to some of his intestines destroying a section. They operated again to remove the dead section of his intestines and he was given a colostomy.

My sister called me to come immediately because his condition was critical. He remained in critical condition for days, and the doctors did not expect him to live. Unfortunately, I had to go back to work. I remember how sad I felt leaving him in the hospital and thinking that I would never see him again. I cried all the way to the airport. When I came home, I sent

$8,000 to pay for his hospital bill. Much to everyone's surprise, my dad recovered and eventually the colostomy was reversed.

Sixteen years later, in March 1996, I received a call from my sister telling me that my father had died peacefully in his sleep. I was retired then and I made immediate reservations to fly to Athens for the funeral. My father was ninety-four years old, and to the day he died he was able to walk and care for his personal needs. I had talked to him only days before he died and he sounded sharp. During his life, along with two wars, he had suffered major illnesses, several operations, cancer, brain surgery, and a colostomy, but he survived everything against all odds. Old age, however, caught up with him, and I was grateful that he had a peaceful death and did not suffer.

Like my mother, my father always wanted to be buried in Vrontama where he had been born and raised. And so it was. The entire family and many friends from Athens accompanied his remains to the church in Vrontama for the funeral and the burial in the village's cemetery next to the white marble vault that we had built for my mother and dedicated to our family. Three years after my father died, we exhumed his remains and placed them in the family vault.

I just could not return to Athens immediately after my father's funeral, so I decided to stay in the village for a few days in order to reminisce with my Uncle John and my other relatives there. Although it was cold, I decided to stay in the house that my father left me which is located next to my grandfather's house. I stayed in Vrontama for a few days and then returned to Athens where I stayed at Alexi's and Potoula's house.

We went through the process of my father's will where he left me three of the six apartments in the building he owned in Neos Cosmos in Athens, along with his house, the aloni and other fields in Vrontama. While I wanted to keep the properties in Vrontama, I decided to sell the three apartments in Athens to my sister's family due to the fact that I was not able to perform the duties of a landlord from the states.

I always had the highest respect and admiration for my dad. I loved both of my parents very much. The only regret I have is that I never told them that enough. May God bless their souls. I hope that I will leave this world with as good a legacy as my parents left.

My Church Community Involvement

Until the early 1970s we went to church in Springfield while visiting with my in-laws on weekends. Once in a while we attended services in the church in Cincinnati. When my Uncle George Manos was diagnosed with cancer, Diane and I decided to attend Sts. Constantine and Helen Greek Orthodox Church in Middletown. This gave us the chance to visit with my uncle and bring him food. After his death, we decided to stay with that church because of the many friends that we and our daughters had there. Cia and Nickie were happy going to Sunday School in that church, and we did not want to uproot them and take them to Cincinnati's church at that time. We attended services in Middletown until 1984.

During the time we attended church there, I was elected to the Parish Council and at the same time as treasurer of the parish, a position I held until the summer of 1984. The church's finances were depleting at a pace greater than its income. Fellow council members Mike Revelos, Al Jones, and I decided that it was time to introduce the community to the Fair Share system of giving. This enabled the church to overcome most of its financial problems.

In 1984 Mike Revelos accepted a job in Germany and moved there with his family. With my uncle gone and now our koumbari moving away, the long driving distance of forty-two miles each way did not seem worthwhile. Although we liked the Middletown parish very much, it was the Sunday visits with Mike and Tina and the children that really drew us to Middletown.

We started attending services at the church in Cincinnati. It was an easy transition for me because I had known Fr. Mitsos, the Cincinnati priest, for several years, and we had developed a friendship long before our family started coming to the Cincinnati church. He appreciated the fact that I had been courteous enough to call him and give him the reasons for our decision to attend services in Middletown.

I transferred my AHEPA membership to the Cincinnati Chapter, and little by little I became known and involved in the community. I met and became good friends with Gus Skufis, Manny Dracakis, John Suhar, Mark Zigoris and several other families. Jim Demetrion and his wife Carole were also members of the Cincinnati Greek community, and we renewed our friendship which had started in Middletown in the fifties. I was elected to the Parish Council, and in 1990 and 1991 I served as president.

In 1988 and in 1989 I was appointed as the general chairman for our annual Panegyri Greek Festival, which is always held in June. This was a huge four-day event, which is now held for only three days, that requires someone with good organizational skills to pull the entire parish together to work towards the same goal. This is sometimes difficult to do because you have to deal with all types of personalities, feelings, egos and work ethics. During my two-year tenure as chairman, we had the best Panegyri Festival up to that time, and our sales surpassed all previous records.

While president of the Parish Council, I consulted with Fr. Mitsos, and with his blessing I tried to promote, through the Parish Council, some changes that would benefit the order during church services, the make-up of the Parish Council and the expansion of the church facilities. The new facilities included a new Sunday school and Greek school wing, more office space, a larger kitchen, a larger Banquet Room, a long hallway next to the Community Room which connects the rear parking lot with the main entrance and can be used as an extension of the Community Room, and an expanded parking lot. The expansion projects carried the cost of over $1,700,000. A Phase IV Committee was appointed to oversee everything from construction to fundraising. All the projects were completed with the support of our priest and the commitment of the parishioners of our church.

After my term on Parish Council was over in January 1992, I had much more free time, so I volunteered to help three elderly ladies by providing transportation to the doctor, to the grocery, to church on Sundays and to any social events sponsored by our church community. All three had come from Geraki, a small village about six kilometers from my hometown, Vrontama. They knew my father from the time they were young girls, and we developed a strong friendship.

Mrs. Viola Christopher, well into her nineties, was the aunt of Christina Geovanes and her sister Nasoula, both in their eighties. Mrs. Christopher was of good financial means. At one of my weekly visits at her assisted living facility, she told me that she wanted to give money to the church for a specific project and asked for my opinion on what that project should be. I told her that in my opinion one project that was needed was the artwork on the ceiling of the church. The other project was the building of a chapel behind the sanctuary. The second idea was immediately dismissed by her, but she liked the first project that I suggested. I informed Mrs. Christopher that if she wanted to proceed any further with this, she would have to present it to the priest and to the Parish Council for their approval. She asked me to take her to the next Parish Council meeting and be her spokesman in presenting her wishes to the council. And so it was.

The project was approved by a narrow margin, and a mosaic artist was commissioned for the job. The artwork was completed within four months after the artist's design was accepted. Mrs. Christopher paid for the entire cost of $545,000. Besides the ceiling artwork, the cost also covered improvements in the lighting and the sound systems. Mrs. Christopher passed away less than a year later and left her legacy in the community as a great benefactress. Her nieces Christina and Nasoula passed away within the next two years, leaving money in their wills to several church organizations and to the Order of AHEPA for a scholarship. I had grown very fond of all three of these ladies and was quite sad to see them go. May God rest their souls.

Opening a New Chapter

My Daughters Move Out and Get Married

When my daughter Cia graduated from college, she convinced me that we should move into a new house in a different neighborhood. We put our house up for sale and started looking for a new one. We looked at several areas of town, but finally decided we would stay in Anderson Township. We found a house we liked, but we had not sold our old one yet, so we waited. As soon as we sold our house, Diane went to see the one we wanted to buy. As luck would have it, it had sold that same day. We had sixty days to find a house. After several weeks of looking with no luck, Diane went to the street we had liked and saw a house that had just been put on the market that day. She called me at work and told me that she found the house that we should buy. After work, we both went to see it and bought it that night. We still live there.

Within a year, Cia told us that she wanted to move out of the house and find an apartment in the Hyde Park area where she could be a little independent from mom and dad. She was working as a social worker and could afford rent and a car payment. She found a good apartment and a roommate and moved out on her own. When Nickie graduated from college and started working at Fidelity Investments, she and Cia moved into another apartment together in Mt. Lookout. We were very proud of the girls for being responsible and financially independent.

Before I realized it, my girls had grown up and were ready to get married. One of Cia's best friends from DePauw introduced her to a fellow graduate student at Harvard University named Thomas S. Souleles from Chicago, Illinois. I met Tom when he came to Cincinnati for a weekend to see Cia. He seemed like a nice young man, and we were happy that Cia had met someone who was well-educated and with a great future. Tom's parents lived in Chicago and were in partnership with their relatives in owning and operating a supermarket. Both parents had come from the Greek province of Achaia and the small town Agios Nicholaos close to Kalavreta, a city known for the start of the Greek War of Independence in 1821. Before Cia and Tom were engaged, I saw Tom again when we both happened to be in Greece vacationing. Tom and one of his cousins were visiting relatives in their parents' village and in Athens when Tom called me and asked if we could meet. My brother-in-law Alexi and I drove to the city and invited them to my sister's house for lunch. My father was still living, and it gave my father and Tom a chance to meet. Later that year, on one of Cia's trips to Chicago, he proposed to her and gave her an engagement ring.

Around the same time, Nickie started dating a very nice young man named John Kahle who also worked at Fidelity. Nickie brought John to see us several times, and Diane and I were very impressed with him. John's parents lived in Boston, but most of his relatives live in California. One morning, I received a call from John asking me to meet him at a restaurant for lunch. There was no doubt in my mind why he wanted me to meet him. I agreed and during lunch he asked me for my Nickie's hand in marriage. John is Catholic, but he was willing to be married in the Greek Church and have their children baptized in our church. Naturally, I gave my blessing. I was so happy that a young man had come to me to ask me for my Nickie's hand in marriage. That really impressed me because I had done the same thing thirty-five years before. John gave an engagement ring to Nickie within days, and all of a sudden both of my daughters were engaged. On one hand, I was happy for my daughters for marrying two wonderful young men, but on the other hand, I felt as though I were losing them and that our relationships would change forever.

Before the rings were on their fingers, the wedding plans had begun. Both Cia and Nickie decided that their weddings were to take place in 1996. Cia's and Tom's wedding was scheduled for July 6, and Nickie's and John's, for October 5. At that time, Diane was working full time as an Administrative Assistant at the Indian Hill Church. Anyone who has planned one wedding can imagine what it must have been like to plan for two weddings three months apart.

Before we even got to the weddings, we had two separate engagement parties of about thirty-five to forty-five people at our home. They gave us the opportunity to meet many of the boys' relatives and friends. Diane did all the preparations and cooking. That was only the beginning. Just trying to schedule the church, the hotel, the band, the florist, the photographer, and the cake for both weddings was a huge challenge. Since we did not have a wedding coordinator and she was the mother of both brides-to-be, Diane had to make all the arrangements and also do all of her office work. To this day I don't know how she was able to make all those arrangements and accompany both girls to look for wedding dresses, invitations, programs, flowers for the church and reception, select the menus, wedding music, trumpeter, limousines, and so much more. I only got involved in tasting the food at the hotels and paying the bills. Actually, I handled the stress very well.

Cia's reception was held at the Omni Netherland, and Nickie's, at the Westin. The receptions were attended by approximately 275 people and to this day, friends and relatives still tell us how classy they were and what a wonderful time they had.

My sister came from Greece to attend both weddings, and our friend Mally, her son Andreas and his wife came from Greece for Nickie's wedding. I was pleased to have them here for the weddings. I could only imagine my mother's happiness if she had been here to see her granddaughters' weddings. The presence of my sister and our friends who came from Greece meant a lot to me because my sister was the only close relative I had from my immediate family. Unfortunately my father had died the prior March. I am positive that if he were still living and in good health, he would have been happy to come to the weddings of both girls.

Almost all of Tom's many aunts, uncles and cousins came from Chicago as well as many of his college and graduate school friends. John's extended family came from California and a large group of Nickie's and John's co-workers came from Fidelity. Both weddings were very elegant and a lot of fun with Greek and American dancing. Both of my girls were beautiful. I was emotional when I walked my daughters down the aisle, but happy knowing that they both were marrying two really wonderful young men.

My Grandchildren

After almost two years of marriage, Cia was expecting our first grandchild. Unfortunately, she had an extremely difficult pregnancy.

She developed static migraines and was hospitalized for several weeks at a time. At one time her migraine lasted non-stop for two months. When Northwestern Hospital said they could not help her, she was the first pregnant woman ever admitted into the Diamond Headache Clinic, which specializes in the most difficult cases of migraines. Diane took a leave of absence from work and spent most of that time in Chicago.

Cia finally gave birth to our first grandchild, Sam, on September 30, 1998. Following the Greek tradition of naming the first boy child after the husband's father, Sam was baptized Sotiri in Sts. Peter and Paul Church in Glenview, Illinois, and the best man at Cia and Tom's wedding, Nick S. Souleles, became Sam's godfather.

Shortly after Sam was born, my good friend Eleftherios Karkadoulias purchased a new car and was awarded a three-day cruise in the Caribbean which he passed on to me. I gave it to Tom and Cia. I thought that it would be good for Cia to get away for a few days after suffering so much during her pregnancy. Diane had taken so much time off work while Cia was pregnant that she could not get off again to go to Chicago to care for Sam. So I volunteered and stayed with baby Sam while his parents went on their cruise. I took care of Sam by myself for four days, and it was one of the best experiences in my life. Some people cannot believe it when they hear that I, at sixty-four years old, took care of a six-week-old baby. While babysitting, I developed a migraine headache. I suffer from terrible migraines. I prayed to God very hard to please make my headache go away so that I could take care of Sam, and thank God it did.

When Sam was about nine months old, I took him for a walk in the stroller to a nearby park. There were several children playing on the path near the entrance, and their mother said to them, "Make room for grandpa to get through." That stands out in my mind as a defining moment for me. That was when I really began to think of myself as a grandpa, a title that I really cherish.

Sam was an exceptionally good, quiet baby, and he has grown into a very good boy. He attends the Latin School, which is a very good private school in Chicago. He loves to read, is a very good thinker and very conscientious. He has the patience to put together Lego sets with hundreds of pieces. He likes to play soccer and tennis and, of course, video games. He also has some very cool dance moves which will come in handy as he approaches his teens.

Cia's next baby was born prematurely on March 11, 2002. Cia had developed undiagnosed pre-eclampsia which is very dangerous for both mother and baby. She had an emergency caesarean while Tom was in Europe on business. Diane and I had been in Chicago, and just when we returned to Cincinnati, we got a call from Cia saying that she was at the hospital and that they were going to operate right away. We immediately drove back to Chicago and went directly at the hospital where we found Cia in very weak condition. Both she and her daughter had come very close to dying. The baby weighed only 2 lbs., 5 oz. and had been growth restricted in the womb.

It soon became evident that the baby had other problems. The next day she was transferred to the Newborn Intensive Care Unit of Children's Hospital where a few days later she was operated on for necrotizing enderocolitis and had a section of her bowel removed. Cia insisted that they operate at midnight. The doctor admitted later that if they had waited until morning, it would have been too late. The baby was too weak to be moved to an operating room, so they operated on her in her room in her isolette. Although she survived the surgery well, she still failed to thrive because of the location of the ileostomy. Diane stayed in Chicago for weeks to help the family. Tom and Cia decided to name the baby Georgia after me, which made me very happy and proud to have one of my grandchildren named after me. Diane went to the hospital every day for a few hours to stay with Georgia and give Cia a chance get out. After three months, Georgia had another operation to reverse the ileostomy and she began to recover. After almost four months in intensive care, Georgia came home weighing about 4 lbs. Cia and Tom asked Nickie to be the godmother.

Georgia is a miracle child. After a shaky start in life, she has now grown into a beautiful and extremely smart little girl. She is vivacious, daring, and very articulate with a mind of her own. Although she loves pretty clothes, perfume and dolls, she loves to play with her brother and cousins and can hold her own with the boys. She, too, attends the Latin School and is an excellent reader. She is very artistic, likes to sing and dance, and plays soccer and tennis. She is my only granddaughter and a source of great joy.

Nickie and John had been married for three years when they had their first baby on December 20, 1999. They decided to name their son Christopher. He was baptized in the Greek Orthodox Church in

Cincinnati and his godfather was Nick M. Revelos, my koumbaro Mike's son who had been their koumbaro.

Christopher was a challenge as a baby, but he has grown into a wonderful, loving boy with a dazzling smile and great zest for life. He loves sports and plays football, basketball and baseball. He is also very good at golf. Diane and I go to see him play, and I get great pleasure in watching him play competitive sports. Although John travels a lot with this work, he loves sports and takes the boys to games, golfing or swimming every weekend. Christopher attends Immaculate Heart of Mary School and is an excellent student, especially in math. Of course, he, too, loves video games.

On October 2, 2003, Nickie and John had their second baby boy whom they named Andrew. He was baptized in our church in Cincinnati and his godmother was Mary Revelos, my koumbaro Mike's daughter. It makes me very happy that the close ties we have with Mike and Tina will continue in our children's generation.

Andrew is naturally athletic and tries to do everything his big brother does. He plays basketball, baseball, and gets lots of practice tackling his brother in preparation for football in the fall. He is friendly, likes to crack jokes and is an excellent student. He, too, is an avid video game player.

None of my grandchildren look alike. Sam looks exactly like me from my tan coloring to his straight, dark hair. He is a Spartan. Christopher looks like his mother. He has the same color hair, even with a little curl, and the same facial features. He even walks like her. Georgia looks like her father, but like Nickie in profile. She has Nickie's hair color and her mother's thick hair and delicate bone structure. Andrew is his own man. He is blond with beautiful blue eyes. He is well-built and his white/blond hair is darkening as he gets older. All my grandchildren are good and well-behaved, and I am very proud to be their grandfather. The most wonderful thing in the world is a hug from my grandchildren.

Cia and her family come to Cincinnati for the Christmas holidays, spring break, and a few weeks in the summer. When they come, Sam, Christopher, Georgia and Andrew enjoy playing together. They seem to get along very well. Watching them play gives me the opportunity to see things through their eyes. I enjoy them when they play and even when they sometimes have conflicts. I always look forward to seeing all four of them together. I feel blessed and thank God for being able to see them grow from one year to the next.

My Involvement with AHEPA Housing

After I transferred from the Middletown chapter to the Cincinnati chapter of AHEPA in 1984, I was elected to several offices and became active on several committees. In the late 1990s, I was elected chapter president succeeding Mark Zigoris. During Mark's and my administrations, we increased the chapter's membership, and our monthly meetings became well-attended and well-organized.

During his presidency, Mark had asked me to spearhead an effort to find a three to four acres lot that would be appropriate for an AHEPA senior citizen apartment building. This was recommended by a group of AHEPANs from Indianapolis who attended one of our meetings and urged us to consider doing this. Since I was retired, I had the time to look for the right type of lot for this project. I searched for over a year without finding anything that would be approved by the United States Housing and Urban Development Department (HUD). The apartments were to be built with grants from HUD. Little by little I became well-educated about all aspects concerning such a project. The chosen location was to be close to churches, medical facilities, banks, drug stores and shopping areas. The tenants of such a facility had to be at least sixty-two years old and their annual income was not to exceed $23,000.

Not being able to find the right location for a reasonable price, I contacted my friend and architect John Suhar who helped me locate a property in Miami Township, a suburb of Milford, Ohio, located northeast of Cincinnati. The property was owned by the mother of a friend of his. However, it was not zoned for a multi-resident building, and we had to jump through several hoops in order to use it for building the senior citizen apartments. One of the things that we had to do was to create a not-for-profit corporation with its own board of directors and officers which would in fact become the owner corporation for the apartment building. I was elected as president. After being rejected the first time we applied, our application to HUD for a grant was finally accepted. The architect supervised the construction bidding and the building construction, while I, with help from my friend Jim Demetrion, handled the legal, consultant and HUD issues. The grant from HUD for the cost of the lot, the building and miscellaneous expenses incurred by the chapter was $3,350,000. The building phase was finished on time. In December

2002, the building was certified for occupancy by Miami Township, and the first residents started to move into the building.

Being the local corporation president, I automatically became a member of the Board of Directors of the AHEPA National Housing Corporation (ANHC) which serves as the sponsor for all such projects in the entire United States. At the 2005 Annual Meeting, I was also elected as a member of the ANHC Executive Board. The Board of Directors of this corporation meets once a year in Indianapolis where the headquarters for the ANHC and the AHEPA Management Company (AMC) are located. Our local corporation has delegated the administration of our building to AMC for a monthly fee which is proportionate to the number of apartments in the building.

In 2003 we applied to HUD and received $3,570,000 for another senior citizen apartment building to be located in Mt. Healthy, Ohio. The process was the same as in our first apartment building, and in May of 2005 the first residents moved in.

Both buildings have a large room called "The AHEPA Room" which can be used by our chapter for its meetings. Since the Mt. Healthy building is only three miles from our church, the chapter made the decision to hold its monthly meetings in that building, and the Daughters of Penelope, AHEPA's women's auxiliary, also decided to meet there.

I personally feel really good for having these two beautiful buildings where senior citizens of limited means can live in a clean and secure environment and enjoy fellowship and friendship with other people their own age. There are a total of ninety-eight apartments in both buildings which are full, and we have many people on the waiting list. I consider this a tribute to AHEPA and a monument to our forefathers who came to their new country in the early 1900s with nothing but the will to work hard, educate their children and make them productive citizens in the new land. Credit must also go to the two local owner corporations which took the initiative to apply and receive government dollars for the two buildings. I cannot think that there is anything more philanthropic than providing a safe and clean environment for seniors of limited means whose rent, in most cases, is subsidized by the government's Housing and Urban Development Department.

At the end of its fiscal year, the ANHC distributes part of the profit that they may have made during the year to several charities while the other half comes back to our Cincinnati AHEPA Philanthropic Foundation.

Because of our corporate ownership of two buildings, the Foundation receives plus or minus $4,000 annually which is distributed to local charities and scholarship foundations.

Life after Retirement

Although my working days ended a little sooner that I had expected, my disciplined saving through the years and some good investments left me fairly comfortable financially, so I did not have to seek another paying position. This gave me the time to take long vacations to Greece visiting friends and relatives and also to be involved with helping other people.

I go back to my own childhood during World War II and the Greek civil war when we had lost everything and went to Athens to save our lives with nothing more than the clothes on our backs. Good people helped us then, and I always remember their kindness and their help. From that time on, I always wanted to give back as much as I could.

As I mentioned in a previous chapter, I helped three older ladies with their errands and later became active in helping senior citizens with housing through my membership in AHEPA. Being involved with the senior housing project is giving me lots of pleasure. How could I not be pleased when during my visits, little old ladies come and give me a hug, thanking me for providing such a nice and secure place for them to live? I am always deeply moved whenever that happens.

After I retired, I went to Greece just about every year to visit my father, my Uncle John in the village, and my sister and her family. I really enjoy visiting Vrontama and seeing some of the people that I still remember from childhood. I always feel a serenity and peace during my visits there. All the bad memories of things that I had experienced during WW II and the Greek civil war have left me, and I now think of all the good memories. I mostly remember the love and affection of my parents and grandparents, my Uncle John and my relatives. I always remember the family gatherings and the happiness and the love that we always felt when we were together. That is what I will always remember for as long as I live.

When I retired, Diane was working full time. I decided that I would learn how to cook. This was a big challenge for me because I had never even poured a cup of coffee let alone brewed one. I collected recipes for food I liked and eventually experimented with my own ideas. Soon I was inviting my friends for lunch that I prepared. Diane loved coming home from work to find dinner ready. Cooking was a great creative outlet for me. However, once Diane retired, I stopped cooking. After all, it really was her responsibility.

On October 4, 2001 I experienced the worst setback to my health. Just when one thinks that he is invincible and can continue to work mentally and physically as hard as he did when he was ten years younger, the good Lord lets him know that he is getting older and should slow down. That is what happened to me. I was in Middletown with Jim and Carole Demetrion attending a meeting in preparation for that city's fall festival when suddenly I felt dizzy, weak and disoriented. I was taken to the Middletown Hospital, and after an hour or so the hospital released me and told me that I had an inner ear problem and that I could drive home to Cincinnati. I could barely walk or see clearly, and they told me I could drive home! It took two people to get me to the car. Mike and Tina Revelos took me to their home where I stayed for two days. At that time, Diane was in Chicago helping Cia and her family and did not know what had happened. After two days, Tina called Diane and told her that I was staying with them because I was not well. A friend of mine from Cincinnati came and took me to my doctor who put me in the hospital immediately and Diane rushed home. The tests indicated that I had suffered a small stroke which was caused by temporary blockage of a small artery in the brain. I had blurry, triple vision and balance problems for several weeks, but eventually my vision stabilized and my balance improved. I had another similar experience called a TIA two years later, but it was not as severe.

I was determined to continue to do the things that I always did, but I learned to slow down and rest as soon as I felt tired. I stopped mowing my lawn and doing heavy yard work that I used to do. I started exercising at a gym three days a week. I continue to have some dizzy spells and at times lose my balance to this day, but I have learned to cope by always being aware of the ground on which I walk. This has not stopped me from my work with the senior housing projects, getting together with friends, and helping others. I believe that this was God's way of telling me to slow down.

Being retired has given me the opportunity to renew old friendships and make new ones. I have become very good friends with Lefteri Karkadoulias who is well-known as an artist who builds bronze statues not only in Cincinnati, but everywhere in the United States. Lefteri and

I were on the same plane to Greece in 1993. We got to know each other and eventually became the best of friends. Several years later when he was getting married, he asked me to be his best man. Unfortunately, after he married, he moved to Dayton, Ohio, but we still remain very close and see each other every week or two.

Several friends and I used to meet regularly at a restaurant owned by Greek friends. Whenever we went to that restaurant, whoever was around from the Greek community would join us. Sometimes, there would be seven or eight men around the table, and the topics of conversation ranged from American and Greek politics, to business, jokes and the church. With both liberals and conservatives in the group, at times there were some heated discussions. That, however, never stopped us from being good friends and always respecting each other's views.

We were all getting along so well that at one of our lunch meetings we decided to take a trip to Las Vegas for four days and try our luck at winning in the casinos. Only one or two of us won a little money, but we all enjoyed the trip and the fun we had for the days we were there. We even drove to see the Hoover Dam which to me by itself was worth the trip. We saw movies and pictures of before, during and after construction and the magnificent engineering that was involved in all building phases. The most fascinating thing that impressed me was that it took only four years to construct this magnificent project. We all returned home with some great memories of the fun and fellowship we enjoyed together in Las Vegas. Unfortunately, in 2001 that restaurant was sold and we lost our gathering place. Some of us continue to get together for lunch and fellowship, but it is not the same.

A few years ago, Jim Demetrion convinced me to join an organization called the Metallic Club. The members of this organization are all men who are retired. Most of these men were professional people: doctors, lawyers, engineers, accountants, etc. The club meets every Friday in one of two church halls from 10 to 11 A.M. Every week we have a speaker who presents and discusses topics of interest to the members. The topics range from World War II and Korean War experiences, to global warming issues, political issues concerning the country, sciences, travels and many others too numerous to mention. In the fall of 2007 I was asked to speak about my experience as a youngster during the German occupation during WW II and the Greek civil war that followed. The club appreciated my speech and asked if I could go into more detail at another meeting. After each meeting, some of us go for lunch and discuss the events of the week and the topic of the day's program.

Trips to China and Alaska

In the summer of 2000, a friend of mine and I decided to take a guided tour of China. We flew to Los Angeles and from there to Beijing with a Chinese airline. We were impressed with the service given to us on the plane and the way the airline attendants treated us on such a long flight. We arrived in Beijing at midnight local time and were taken to our hotel where we met the rest of the people in our group. The hotel was comparable to a good American hotel, except that the water was not drinkable. We drank the two complimentary bottles of water that the hotel provided, and the next morning I walked to a small grocery where I purchased a few bottles to have in our room.

The next day we were picked up by an air-conditioned bus with a Chinese guide, who spoke very little English, and toured the city, stopping for lunch at a totally Chinese restaurant that did not serve us individually. Instead the waiters put a variety of dishes on a Lazy Susan in the middle of the table, and the people at the table served themselves. I guess the food that we were served during our entire stay in China was fair, but I would take the Chinese-American cuisine any time before the native cuisine. On our first day we visited Tiananmen Square and the Forbidden City. In the evening we attended a Chinese ballet performance, which did not at all resemble ballet as we know it in America. The Chinese ballet, in my opinion, resembled actors and actresses telling a story while performing acrobatic moves.

The next day we were taken to the Great Wall where we were encouraged to walk as far as we wanted on the top of it. That was not an easy task. I walked several sections of the wall. Walking uphill was actually easier than coming back down again because the surface of the walking area was quite slippery, and I certainly did not want to slip and fall. My friend climbed the stairs to the top of the Wall, but that was as far as he went. The commerce around the base of the Wall was unbelievable. Hundreds of small retail shops, one after the other, and walking vendors lined both sides of the street hawking their goods. If you approached one of them, the merchant did not let you leave until he finished lowering the price enough for you to buy an item. Price bargaining was their way of selling their goods and their customers followed suit.

After three days in Beijing, we embarked on a large Chinese riverboat for a four-day cruise on the Yangtze River. It is the dirtiest river that I have ever seen, but since I was on the boat, it did not bother me at all. One of the places that we visited during the cruise was the Three Gorge hydroelectric project which, when completed, will be the biggest project of its kind in the world. There must have been a million men and women working on that project. A bus took us from the boat to this project. It stopped on a road which was far above the level where the work was being done. People looked like thousands of ants moving around doing their work. We visited several cities during the cruise where we were able to walk around and do some shopping.

For the rest of our trip we flew to several other major cities. I was really impressed with the Chinese airlines because they were really great in service and politeness. In the various cities during our trip, we stayed in really nice hotels where we still had to drink water from bottles. In Shanghai we actually stayed in a Holiday Inn in which we were able to have American food for dinner. While in Shanghai, we visited the center of the city, and what impressed me the most was the European style of business buildings and hotels. We were told that in years past the residents of the city were mostly Europeans who engaged in commerce from the port of Shanghai. In those cities we visited factories, large and small, and everyone we met was friendly and very helpful.

The last city that we visited in China was Hong Kong where we stayed two days. I took a walk to the area of Hong Kong which is famous for tailoring a custom-made suit or shirt within hours. There is a street with tailor shops on each side where the tailors show the fabrics and ask you to come in and be measured for a suit. I, at that time, had enough suits and did not have an interest in buying another one, but I just wanted to walk that famous street and observe the different types of commerce that were taking place.

After two days in Hong Kong, we were driven to the airport, which sits on a man-made island about an hour from the city, and left again with a Chinese airline for Los Angeles. It was a very interesting trip because that was the first time that I had visited a Communist country. I saw that the Chinese people were hard-working and always trying to sell us items with the good merchandising practice of first asking higher prices for their goods than the amount for which they eventually sold them. Commerce was alive and well during our visit, and it has become even greater now. When I saw what was happening then, I just knew that China was to become a large economic power in the not-so-distant future.

Two years after the China trip, my friend Mark Zigoris talked me into going on a seven-day cruise in Alaska. I had had my stroke by then and was not as steady on my feet as I used to be, but I really wanted to see Alaska. We flew to Vancouver, Canada, and after visiting the city for a day, we embarked on the ship that took us to Juneau, the capitol of Alaska. There we spent half of the day touring the city and window shopping at the many tourist shops. I learned that the only way to get to Juneau is by sea or by plane. There are no trains or roads for automobiles to or from the city. I was really surprised that any American state capital was restricted to only air or water transportation. On our way to Glacier Bay, we stopped at Ketchikan, another Alaskan city, for sightseeing and window shopping.

When someone thinks about Alaska, they think of ice and much snow during the winter. That, to my surprise, is not true. Some of the Alaskan cities along the coast have a tremendous amount of rain during the entire year, but not too much snow or extreme cold. On the contrary, if you exclude the rain, their winters are mild compared to some of the winters that we have in Ohio and other states. The farther north we went, the guides told us that the daylight hours during the winter months are non-existent if not limited to only an hour or so during the entire day. This has resulted in a higher than normal suicide rate than in the rest of the country. The terrain in the cities we visited is mountainous with very little soil for cultivating because of the solid granite below the surface. It is very difficult to bury people in that kind of terrain because it is almost impossible to dig a grave through the underlying granite unless they use dynamite, which is very expensive for most of the residents. Because of this, most of the people are cremated.

The most challenging part of the trip for me was a rather long, three-mile hike uphill through the wilderness. I bought a tall, strong walking stick and managed pretty well, especially considering my balance problems. It was an exhausting hike, but fortunately someone met us at the end of the hike, and we rode an inflated boat back downstream on a beautiful, clean river. While this trip helped me learn a few things about Alaska and its people, the most memorable part for me was the relaxation, great food and the people that I had the pleasure of meeting on the boat.

I am, by nature, a people-oriented person and I enjoy meeting new people and learning about them.

America Then and Now

I arrived in the United States on September 27, 1950 not knowing the language and without a penny in my pocket. I had one thing in my favor: the will and ability to adjust in my new environment and make the best of the situations in which I would find myself. All the relatives and friends that I met in America could not have been nicer to me. It was, however, when I started going to an American high school and later to college that I realized that this was indeed a special country in which to live.

While in high school, one of the courses that I had to take besides English, Math, History, etc, was a course called Civics. I was really happy to take this course because it taught me about our government and how this nation works. I understood the Constitution and the three different branches of government as all my classmates did at that time. I quickly realized that I was in a country of laws that protected its citizens who obeyed its laws. When I was deported and returned to Greece to come back as a student, I knew the law that I had broken and why I had to go back.

We now have young and older adults who do not know anything about our history and do not even know the three branches of our government and their responsibilities. Young kids in high school cannot name the leaders in Congress. People blame the government for everything that happens in their lives instead of looking within themselves for answers and for help. Some schools are more interested in promoting self-esteem in children instead of teaching what they need to know to succeed in life.

In Greece, boys and girls attended separate high schools which made it impossible to have any fraternization between boys and girls of the same age. In the American high school, I was really surprised to see girls attending the same classes with the boys and actually being friends. Knowing that I had come from Greece with very limited knowledge of English, both boys and girls came to me and helped me with my lessons and even helped me meet other students. Later, when I discovered the concept of going on a date with a girl, I had to go to the girl's house and meet the parents before she walked out of the house. The dates were to go to a basketball or a football game and later to a hamburger place for a hamburger, French fries and a milk shake. When I took the girl home, if she agreed, I gave her a goodnight kiss, but never on the first date.

Before our first class in high school started, the principal announced through the public address system that we had to recite a generic prayer and the Pledge of Allegiance. It was a simple, short prayer thanking God for his blessings and the health of our families and our nation. Prayers in school are now something of the past, even if students want to congregate privately on the school grounds and pray by themselves. The Ten Commandments have been taken out of schools and public buildings. It is no wonder that some school children in public schools do not know the boundaries of morality or the difference between good and bad, honor and dishonor, law and lawlessness.

In recent years, I have noticed that some high school students have abandoned certain elements of self-discipline and respect and have eliminated many of the boundaries that were required in years past in school attire. I see students of both genders wearing clothes that years ago would have been considered offensive by society, by the school and even by other students. It seems that the boundaries of decency have been crossed, but I hope not forever.

Watching television was a luxury not a necessity. In fact, my aunt with whom I stayed during my school years did not have a television until 1952. If there was a program that my aunt and I wanted to see, we were always invited to visit with the Kilavos family and watch "I Love Lucy" and other programs at their house. Television programs were always programs for the entire family. Today there are hundreds of television stations which show a great variety of programs and information. There are many programs that are suitable for all ages. Unfortunately, some of the programs have lowered the morals of our country with commercials for male and female enhancement drugs, a great deal of violence, foul language, nudity, and sex. The parents of children are now constantly obligated to closely monitor what their children are watching and find the right words to explain to them some of the things that they now hear and see on television.

Another major change in American life today is the wide range of computer technology. When I started working with computers they were so large that they filled a whole room. Today handheld devices can give instant access to news, entertainment, books and communication.

In the fifties and early sixties, the political arena was filled with ladies and gentlemen who mostly worked together for the benefit of all Americans. Although both parties had their differences and their own convictions on the floor of both houses of Congress, they discussed the issues while respecting the views of their opposition. Now we have politicians whose first priority is to be re-elected. The civility in both houses of Congress has been put aside in order to make room for programs that are clearly not part of our Constitution. In time of war, some politicians do not hesitate to call a war lost while our men and women are still fighting, putting their lives in jeopardy to protect us. With all our imperfections as a nation, however, America is still the best country in the world and will continue to be the "shining city on the hill" for the world to see and admire.

On September 11, 2001, I was visiting my aunt in Vrontama. She woke me from my afternoon nap to come to the television. I watched the attack on America on CNN. There I was in the village of my youth where I had experienced WW II and the Greek civil war, and now I was watching my adopted country under attack. As a boy I heard war news on a secret radio that someone had to keep cranking to make it work. Now as an old man in that same village I could see my country being attacked in color on TV. War is the same in any medium. It was a very emotional day. I even thought about going home and enlisting. Then I remembered that I was sixty-seven years old and the army would not want me. I still get emotional when I think of that day.

Reflections on My Life

Now that I am in my seventies and thinning, white hair has replaced the thick, black hair that I once had, I look back on my life trying to think of things that I would or could have done differently. I can honestly say that if I were to live my life all over again, there would be very few changes that I would make. These are changes that do not reflect the struggle for survival and things that were beyond my ability to control in the war years or the pain of homesickness and the loneliness I felt at the beginning of my life in America away from the country and family I loved. All of the above have made me a much stronger person, and I believe I have become a man that can face life and the world much more realistically and with more courage than someone who did not grow up under the stressful situations that I did. I have learned to accept people for who they are and reject not the people, but the ideas they may have about me, my family and even the country that I love so much: the United States of America.

This is the country that presented me with opportunities to work and to live. Because I lived in America, I was able to help my family in Greece financially. Although I went to college and I believe that I did a good job in my work and supported my family well with the means available to me, I always thought that there was something more that I wanted. That was a more flexible mind to understand not only the members of my family and friends better, but also my co-workers. In my younger days, I used to go after what I wanted as long as in my opinion it was the right thing to do and in the process disregarded objections from others. In retrospect, I think I would have done much better if I had considered other peoples' feelings and their ideas instead of pushing my ideas and my proposals over their objections which sometimes deserved consideration.

I did not realize until it was too late in my life that being a people-oriented person, I should have chosen a career totally different from the one I had. My first choice would have been that of having my own business where I could have made my own business decisions and dealt with people on a daily basis. A store owner where people came to buy furniture, equipment, supplies or even a good restaurant would be something that I would have liked to pursue. Another profession that I would have chosen is that of a company representative selling its products: machinery, packaging equipment and material, etc. All of the above would have suited my personality. Any of that type of business would have been somewhat risky, but working in the corporate environment and being compensated fairly well for my work presented me with security especially after I was married and had a family to support.

I would especially like to ask my grandchildren to go through this book once in a while to the chapter entitled "The Long Goodbye" where I have written the advice my father wrote for me in the small 1950 agenda book the day that I left home to come to the United States. If they read, understand, and follow those simple rules, there is nothing that can keep them from being successful in life and being good and productive citizens of this great county in which we live.

I had a great family, relatives and friends in Greece and here. I am married to a good wife and have watched my two, wonderful daughters become kind, thoughtful, intelligent women who contribute to the society in which they live. They married good men and gave us four wonderful grandchildren to love and adore. I have managed to do things that I wanted to do in my retirement. I live in the greatest country in the world and have fulfilled my wish and determination to give back to society in ways that I am able to do so. I cannot think of anything that would have made my life any better. I am indeed a blessed man.

My fiancée Diane   Diane's parents
1964   Steve and Domina Babalis

Our wedding 1964
Uncle George, Mary Kara, Diane, me, Mom, my cousin Georgia

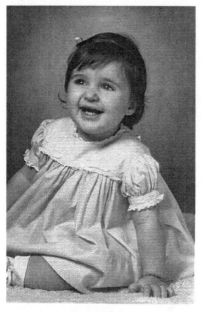

Cia 1968

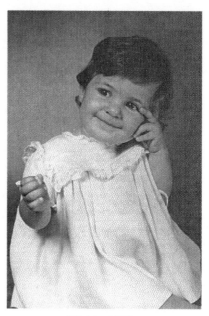

Nickie 1970

Drackett Spring Dance

My father's first trip to America with
Mom and Potoula 1972

My parents in America 1972

My family at Potoula's house in Athens 1978

Cia and Tom Souleles
July 6, 1996

Nickie and John Kahle
October 5, 1996

My girls are mothers
Nickie with Christopher, Cia with Sam

Cia's children, Georgia and Sam

Nickie's children, Andrew and Christopher

The house my father built next to Grandfather
Karampas's house in Vrontama

My parents' burial place in Vrontama

Grandfather Lambros's house where I was born in Kosma

View of Kosma from my grandfather's house

Teaching Systems at
Miami University 1980

I love teaching

Koumbari and best friends,
Mike and Tina Revelos

Good friend since my first days
in America, Jim Demetrion

Friends forever—Jim and Mary Kilavos

Friends forever—Becky and George Pulos

Good friends since high school,
George and Georgia Kilavos

Good friends since coming to America,
Andy and Mary Skalkos

Our friend and my dentist,
Mally Simonetos

Gaby Simonetos, me and Alexi at Spetses

Father Mitsos and the Parish Council 1990

My koumbari and good friends:
Mike Revelos, George Kacos, and Leftheri Karkadoulias

My friends 2000
1st row, l-r: Jim Demetrion, Leftheri Karkadoulias,
George N. Revelos, George Poulos, Mike Revelos
2nd row, l-r: Nick Revelos, me, Art Goldstein, Chris Revelos,
Charlie Revelos, Nick Parthenakis, Jim Kilavos, George C. Revelos

Weekly lunch with friends 2009
Mark Zigoris, Peter Seitanakes, Leftheri Karkadoulias,
John Kanelos, Manny Dracakis, Jim Demetrion, George Christy and me

With my father in Athens 1988

With Potoula and her son John

Great Wall of China 2000

Glacier Bay in Alaska 2002

My family

CPSIA information can be obtained at www.ICGtesting.com
Printed in the USA
BVOW041212070413

317511BV00001B/58/P